RECIPROCAL ENFORCEMENT:

A Practical Guide to Magistrates' Courts' Jurisdiction & Procedure in International Domestic Proceedings

DIBB LUPTON & CO

LITG./BB

RECIPROCAL ENFORCEMENT

A Practical Guide to Magistrates' Courts' Jurisdiction & Procedure in International Domestic Proceedings

Desmond A.G. James
With a Foreword by Dewi E. Davies, LL.B.,
Solicitor, Clerk to the Pembrokeshire
Justices

Chichester
BARRY ROSE PUBLISHERS LTD.

Published by
Barry Rose Publishers Ltd.
Chichester, West Sussex.

Printed in Great Britain by
Commercial Print Services
Portsmouth, Hampshire.

CONTENTS

FOREWORD

In the league of judicial tribunals, the magistrates' court must surely be the one which enjoys the greatest variety of Court business. Of such business, none can be so complicated and demanding as those domestic proceedings which contain an "international element". To fully understand such matters is truly to belong to the few. One of the few is the author of this treatise — my Deputy Clerk, Desmond A.G. James.

I consider it to be a great privilege to be granted this opportunity of introducing the reader of this publication both to the subject matter of the text and to the author.

The subject matter is as old as man himself. Throughout his history, man has strived to build his communal relationships upon the corner-stone of the "family-unit". His basic sense of belonging is first to his family, and extended therefrom to his immediate local community. In more recent times, this sense of belonging has been given a more rigid structure; man now also belongs to a particular country or state. His rights and duties are almost exclusively governed by the laws of his country or state.

Within this framework it is a relatively simple matter for each country or state to develop its own laws to regulate the rights and duties of the parties to a contract of marriage. Further, within its own territorial boundaries, each country or state can regulate the enforcement of the orders made by its own courts of law.

In recent decades however, man has become more mobile and international in his outlook. In consequence, difficulties arise when matrimonial disputes are not contained within "national" boundaries; the parties to the dispute do not both reside within the jurisdiction of the tribunal which determines the issue. The procedures for dealing with such disputes have therefore necessitated agreement on an international basis.

International domestic proceedings have now become commonplace in the Magistrates' Courts of this country. Certain courts, of course, have greater experience than others in this field. The physical location of foreign military establishments, of harbours and ports within the jurisdictional area of the Court determines, to a very large extent, the volume of work to be entertained.

This 'international element' in domestic proceedings concerns not only those of us employed in the Magisterial service but equally concerns officers of the Department of Health and Social Security; officers of the County Treasurer's Department; solicitors in private practice — all of whom may be called upon to take part in the conduct of proceedings before the Magistrates' Court. It is to all such persons that this publication extends the expert's hand to guide them through the minefield of legislation, rules and regulations. The need for this practical guide can only be measured by the vast number of "enquiries" that the author receives on this subject on a weekly basis.

The author, Desmond A.G. James, has over thirty-seven years experience in Magisterial law. He began his distinguished service at the Haverfordwest Court in 1946. Thereafter, he spent a period of ten years at the Barry Magistrates' Courts from 1948 to 1958 — and then returned to his native Pembrokeshire.

During these years, Desmond James has made 'domestic proceedings' —

particularly international domestic proceedings — his own special subject. His knowledge and experience in this field defies comparison. I am confident in the view that the reader will find this 'practical guide' to be a most reliable and useful companion.

I have personally enjoyed the benefit of the author's expertise over a number of years. It would have been rather selfish of me not to have made some effort to share that experience with others. That is why I prevailed upon Desmond James to publish this work.

I commend this publication to all as a practical guide that should serve the user as a standard work on this subject for many years to come.

Dewi E. Davies   July 1984
Clerk to the Justices,
Foley House,
Goat Street,
Haverfordwest,
Dyfed.

PREFACE

From time to time, one meets with the problem as to whether or not a remedy is available where a liable relative has moved overseas, or perhaps, to another country within the United Kingdom.

If a remedy is available, what is the procedure to be followed in order to secure relief by way of enforcing maintenance obligations?

It is hoped that this guide will provide a quick and reliable answer to the above questions.

In the 37 years I have worked in a magistrates' clerk's office, I have prepared the documents in many overseas maintenance cases, and, in my early days, I had many such cases sent back to me by the experts in the Home Office because I had overlooked, or failed to comply with, some provision or other. I hope that this Guide will help the reader to avoid some of the pitfalls which I at first encountered.

I must emphasize that this Guide is in no way an academic treatment of the subject, nor does it pretend to be. Reference should always be made, where necessary, to the appropriate statute, modification order or rules.

The mountain of Home Office circulars going back over many years has proved to be invaluable in the preparation of this Guide — it would not have been possible to prepare it without constant reference to them.

I wish to express my especial thanks and gratitude to the officials in the Home Office for the help which they have given me in the preparation of this Guide, for their many helpful suggestions, and also for their unfailing courtesy. They read my initial manuscript and made many suggestions for improvement, which must have imposed an additional burden upon them on top of their normal workload. I must stress however that any errors or inaccuracies in this Guide are mine and mine alone.

I would like to put on record my deep appreciation to Mr. Dewi Davies, LL.B., Solicitor and Clerk to the Pembrokeshire Justices for his many helpful suggestions, and for the fact that he was always ready to sit down and discuss some difficult point and offer advice, no matter how busy he was. Without Mr. Dewi Davies' encouragement, this Guide would never have been written. I would also wish to express my appreciation to the Publishers for their patience and help — and in particular for the preparation of the index to this Guide.

My thanks also to Mr. Peter Humphries, my friend and colleague in the Magistrates' Clerk's Office at Haverfordwest for typing the major part of the first manuscript prepared by me.

DESMOND A.G. JAMES
Deputy Clerk to the Pembrokeshire Justices,
92 Bush Street,
Pembroke Dock.
Dyfed.

July 1984

INTRODUCTION

The overseas and United Kingdom cross-border arrangements for the making and enforcement of maintenance orders and claims for maintenance may be briefly summarised in the following categories:

1. Reciprocal arrangements affecting recognition and enforcement between England/Wales and Scotland and Northern Ireland.
2. Reciprocal arrangements with Commonwealth countries under the Maintenance Orders (Facilities for Enforcement) Act 1920.
3. Reciprocal arrangements with Foreign, Commonwealth and E.E.C. countries under the Maintenance Orders (Reciprocal Enforcement) Act 1972.

The Maintenance Orders (Facilities for Enforcement) Act 1920 will, in time, become obsolete, by reason of the countries designated by Orders under that Act becoming countries designated in Orders under the 1972 Act.

The countries to which the 1972 Act applies may be sub-divided into the following categories:

1. Reciprocating countries and territories under Part I of the Act.
2. Convention States under Part II of the Act.
3. Hague Convention countries to which Part I of the Act applies by means of the Reciprocal Enforcement of Maintenance Orders (Hague Convention Countries) Order 1979 and subsequent orders.
4. The Republic of Ireland — There is a special arrangement whereby Part I of the 1972 Act is modified by the Reciprocal Enforcement of Maintenance Orders (Republic of Ireland) Order 1974.
5. The majority of the States of the United States of America in respect of which Part II of the 1972 Act has been modified by the Recovery of Maintenance (United States of America) Order 1979 and one subsequent order.
6. Certain countries which are both Convention countries under Part II and Hague Convention countries to which the modified form of Part I applies and where the applicant elects under which part of the Act proceedings will be commenced.

Before the passing of the Maintenance Ordes (Facilities for Enforcement) Act 1920, enforcement of English and Welsh maintenance orders overseas was not possible.

The Summary Jurisdiction (Process) Act 1881 provided for certain limited enforcement within the various jurisdictions of the British Islands, but the passing of the Maintenance Orders Act 1950 made complete recognition and enforcement of maintenance orders between England, Wales, Scotland and Northern Ireland possible for the first time.

The provisions of Part I of the 1950 Act conferred a general or blanket jurisdiction upon the English and Welsh Courts to entertain applications for relief. However, by today, the majority of that 1950 legislation has been repealed and the provisions conferring jurisdiction upon the English and Welsh courts are no longer to be found in one statute. The same or similar provisions have been re-enacted in a number of later statutes; each Act conferring jurisdiction to deal with its own particular provisions for relief.

1. RECIPROCAL ARRANGEMENTS WITH SCOTLAND AND NORTHERN IRELAND

The following are extracts from some of the statutes under which magistrates' courts in England and Wales at present derive jurisdiction in maintenance claims involving persons resident in Scotland and Northern Ireland. It is under these statutes that the majority of claims will be made in the magistrates' courts.

MAINTENANCE ORDERS ACT 1950. s.3(1)

Affiliation Orders — An English Court has jurisdiction in proceedings under the Affiliation Proceedings Act 1957, s.44 of the National Assistance Act 1948 and s.19 of the Supplementary Benefits Act 1976 for an affiliation order against a man residing in Scotland or Northern Ireland if the act of intercourse resulting in the birth of the child or any act of intercourse between the parties which may have resulted therein took place in England. **Section 3(2).** Where the mother of a child resides in Scotland or Northern Ireland and the person alleged to be the father of the child in England, a magistrates' court appointed for the Commission Area in which the person alleged to be the father resides shall have jurisdiction in proceedings by the mother for an affiliation order against him under the Affiliation Proceedings Act 1957.

MAINTENANCE ORDERS ACT 1950. S.4.

Contribution Orders (1) An English court has jurisdiction in proceedings against a person residing in Scotland or Northern Ireland
- (a) for an order under s.43 of the National Assistance Act 1948 (recovery from spouses or parents of sums given in respect of assistance under that Act)
- (b) for an order under s.18 of the Supplementary Benefits Act 1976 (recovery of expenditure on supplementary benefits from persons liable to maintenance).

(2) A Court in England by which an Order has been made under the said s.43 or s.18 shall have jurisdiction by or against a person residing in Scotland or Northern Ireland for the revocation, revival or variation of that order.

GUARDIANSHIP OF MINORS ACT 1971

Section 15(3). A county court or magistrates' court shall not have jurisdiction under this Act in any case where the respondent or any of the respondents resides in Scotland or Northern Ireland
(a) except in so far as such jurisdiction may be exercisable by virtue of the following provisions of this section, or
(b) unless a summons or other originating process can be served and is served on the respondent or, as the case may be, on the respondents in England or Wales.
(4) An order under this Act giving the legal custody of a minor to a person resident in England or Wales whether with or without an order requiring payments to be made towards the minor's maintenance, may be made, if one parent resides in Scotland or Northern Ireland and the other parent and

the minor in England or Wales by a magistrates' court appointed for the commission area in which the other parent resides.

(5) It is hereby declared that a magistrates' court has jurisdiction

    (a) in proceedings under this Act by a person residing in Scotland or Northern Ireland against a person residing in England or Wales for an order relating to the legal custody of a minor (including an Order requiring payments to be made towards the minor's maintenance)

    (b) in proceedings by or against a person residing in Scotland or Northern Ireland for the revocation, revival or variation of any such order.

(6) Where proceedings for an order under s.9(1) of this Act relating to the legal custody of a minor are brought in a magistrates' court by a person residing in Scotland or Northern Ireland, the Court shall have jurisdiction to make any order in respect of the minor under that section on the application of the respondent in the proceedings.

DOMESTIC PROCEEDINGS AND MAGISTRATES' COURTS ACT 1978

Section 24(1). It is hereby delcared that any jurisdiction conferred on a magistrates' court by virtue of

s.20 (variation, revival and revocation of orders for periodical payment) or

s.21 (variation and revocation of orders relating to the custody of children) of this Act is exercisable notwithstanding that the proceedings are brought by or against a person residing outside England and Wales.

Section 30(3). In relation to an application for an order under this part of this Act (other than an application in relation to which jurisdiction is exercisable by virtue of s.24 of this Act) the jurisdiction conferred by subs.1 above

    (a) shall be exercisable notwithstanding that the respondent resides in Scotland or Northern Ireland if the applicant resides in England and Wales and the parties last ordinarily resided together as man and wife in England and Wales, and

    (b) it is hereby declared to be exercisable where the applicant resides in Scotland or Northern Ireland if the respondent resides in England and Wales.

CHILD CARE ACT 1980. s.55

(1) A magistrates' court shall have jurisdiction in proceedings against a person residing in Scotland or Northern Ireland for a contribution order under s.47 of this Act or an arrears order under s.51 of this Act.

(2) A magistrates' court by which an order has been made under ss.47 or 51 of this Act shall have jurisdiction in proceedings by or against a person residing in Scotland or Northern Ireland for the revocation, revival or variation of that order.

(3) A magistrates' court shall have jurisdiction in proceedings against a man residing in Scotland or Northern Ireland for an affiliation order under s.50 of this Act if the act of intercourse resulting in the birth of the child or any act of intercourse between the parties which may have resulted therein took place in England or Wales.

Section 46(1). It is hereby declared that any jurisdiction conferred on a magistrates' court by virtue of this Part is exercisable notwithstanding that the proceedings are brought by or against a person residing outside England and Wales.

Note:- Part 11 consists of ss.33 to 46 of the above Act, which are not yet in force, but the Government has announced its intention to implement them towards the end of 1984.

2. **Service of Process Leading to the Making of Orders.**

    Section 15 of the Maintenance Orders Act 1950 provides the machinery whereby process originating in England and Wales may be served in Scotland and Northern Ireland and vice versa. This section applies equally to summonses for variation as to original Orders.

3.   Summonses issued under this section in England and Wales must be sent to the appropriate sheriff clerk in Scotland or, in Northern Ireland, to the appropriate clerk of petty sessions, with a request that the summons be endorsed in accordance with the said s.15, authorizing service in Scotland or Northern Ireland as the case may be. In Scottish cases, it is advisable to ask the sheriff clerk to return the summons, duly endorsed, and to supply the name and address of a process server who will undertake service. The summons can then be sent to the solicitor for the complainant, with the name of the process server, with a request that the solicitor arranges with the process server for the summons to be served. In so doing, the magistrates' clerk does not become responsible for payment of the process server's fee. In Northern Irish cases, the clerk of petty sessions will, in most cases, arrange for service, and the service fee in most instances is either small or none at all. Summonses must be served personally and a declaration by the process server made before a justice of the peace, resident magistrate or sheriff must be endorsed on the summons or attached thereto. In all cases, it is advisable to set the hearing well in advance to enable the above formalities to be complied with.

4.   Incoming summonses from Northern Ireland and Initial writs from Scotland must be endorsed by a justice of the peace authorizing service in England and Wales. Sometimes the local police are helpful in serving Scottish initial writs and Northern Irish summonses. Occasionally such writs or summonses are received from local solicitors acting as agents for Scottish or Northern Irish solicitors. In the latter event, the writ or summons, after endorsement in accordance with s.15, can be returned to the local solicitors for service, and who, in turn, will return the writ or summons to the Scottish or Northern Irish authorities. Where no local solicitor is acting as agent, the summons or writ, duly endorsed authorizing service, together with a declaration of the personal service of the summons or writ by a police officer is then returned to the clerk of the originating court. The declaration of service must be made before a justice of the peace. Where it is not possible to obtain the services of the local police to serve the writ or summons, it is better to return the summons to the originating court, after endorsement in accordance with the said s.15, and ask that court to arrange for service of the document. The originating court can be informed, at the same time, of the name and address of a process server who will undertake service of the document in England or Wales.

5.   Where the respondent is resident in Scotland or Northern Ireland and the complainant in England and Wales, it should be particularly noted that jurisdiction of the English and Welsh Courts is only exercisable in England and Wales, where:

      (1) In husband and wife proceedings, the parties last ordinarily resided together as man and wife in England or Wales. (Domestic Proceedings and Magistrates' Courts Act 1978, s.30(3)).

      (2) In affiliation proceedings, if the act of intercourse resulting in the birth of the child, or any act of intercourse between the parties which may have resulted therein took place in England or Wales. (Maintenance Orders Act 1950, s.3).

It is important, therefore, that a complaint for an original order where the respondent resides in Northern Ireland or Scotland should contain a declaration in the form of either (1) or (2) above as the case may be. The fact is then expressed in the summons issued upon the complaint. If the summons does not contain the required clause, the Scottish or Northern Irish courts may refuse to endorse it for service on the ground that it does not show jurisdiction on the face of it.

6.   Once the summons is endorsed for service, and served personally, and the English or Welsh court satisfied of these facts, the court is then seized of the matter, and will hear and determine the complaint in accordance with the law of England and Wales. If, however, the respondent fails to appear in answer to the summons, s.15(5) of the Maintenance Orders Act 1950 expressly prohibits the issue of a warrant of arrest. The court must, therefore, hear and determine the complaint in the absence of the respondent.

7.   **Registration of English and Welsh Orders in Scotland and Northern Ireland, and vice versa, for enforcement.**

         Section 16 of the Maintenance Orders Act 1950 sets out the maintenance orders which are enforceable under the Section in the various jurisdictions of the United Kingdom. In so far as the magistrates' courts are concerned, generally speaking, these orders are husband and wife maintenance orders, maintenance orders under the Guardianship of Minors Acts 1971 and 1973, affiliation orders, contribution orders for maintenance of children in local authority care and liable relative orders under s.43 of the National Assistance Act 1948 and s.18 of the Supplementary Benefits Act 1976, and equivalent orders under Scottish and Northern Irish law. Enforcement is to be effected by registering the order in the Court having jurisdiction in that part of the United Kingdom where the respondent appears to be. Superior court orders are to be registered in courts having equivalent jurisdiction in the part of the United Kingdom where the respondent resides, and orders made in courts of summary jurisdiction are to be registered in courts of summary jurisdiction. Thus, where an order is made in an English or Welsh magistrates' court, it must be registered in a petty sessions court in Northern Ireland or a sheriff court in Scotland. Application to register a county court order in Scotland or Northern Ireland should, therefore, be made to the registrar of the county court.

8.   **Procedure upon Applications for Registration**

         Rule 2 of the Maintenance Orders Act 1950 (Summary Jurisdiction) Rules 1950, sets out the procedure to be followed in relation to applications for registration of maintenance orders in Scotland and Northern Ireland. The application may be made by, or on behalf of, the person entitled to the payments either orally, or in writing. The application must be made to a justice of the peace for the same place as the court which made the order. Upon it appearing to the justice hearing the application that:

1. the respondent is residing in Scotland or Northern Ireland, as the case may be; and

2. that it is convenient that the order should be enforced there,

the justice shall cause the clerk to the justices to send to the sherrif clerk, or clerk of petty sessions, as the case may be, for the area where the respondent appears to reside:

1. A certified copy of the maintenance order,

2. A certificate or arrears, or statutory declaration (if any),

3. If no statutory declaration has been lodged, written notice of the address of the person liable to make payments under the order.

If the applicant does not appear in person to make the application for registration of the order, there must accompany the written application, a statutory declaration which shall contain:

(a) the address of the person liable to make payments under the order,

(b) the reason why it is convenient that the order should be enforced in Scotland or in Northern Ireland,

(c) unless a certificate of arrears, signed by the justices' clerk is lodged, the amount of the arrears under the order

(d) a statement that the order is not already registered under Part II of the Maintenance Orders Act 1950.

9. **Recording of Registrations and Functions of Justices' Clerk Following Registration**

A memorandum of any application for registration of an order must be entered in the court register. Similarly, when notice has been received from the clerk of petty sessions, or sheriff clerk, to the effect that registration has been effected, this fact must also be recorded in the court register. The entries must be signed by the justices' clerk. It is good practice to distinguish these entries by recording the fact that the entries are made in accordance with the rules of 1950 referred to above. By virtue of s.19 of the Maintenance Orders Act 1950, when an order has been registered, any provision that payments under the order shall be made through the justices' clerk shall cease to have effect while the order remains so registered. The justices' clerk, will, therefore, be unable to assist the complainant in the enforcement of the order. Complainants may, however, be advised to write to the clerk of petty sessions in Northern Ireland, who will take proceedings in his own name for enforcement. In Scotland, where there are no "Collecting Officers" she should be advised to consult a solicitor, either locally or in Scotland. Legal Aid is available in Scotland for enforcement purposes.

10. **Re-registration in Magistrates' Courts under the Maintenance Orders Act 1958 of Scottish and Northern Irish High Court Orders Already Registered in the English High Court under the Maintenance Orders Act 1950.**

The above scheme came into operation on January 1 1981 by bringing fully into force s.3 of the Administration of Justice Act 1977 and sch.3 thereof. Generally speaking, orders of the Court of Session in Edinburgh and the High Court of Northern Ireland which have been registered in the High Court in England under the Maintenance Orders Act 1950 may be re-registered in a magistrates' court in England or Wales. Upon the re-registration taking place, the order will then be registered in both courts, although enforcement will be by the court of re-registration. The High Court will be precluded from enforcing it while the order remains registered under the Maintenance Orders Act 1958 in the magistrates' court. The re-registration may be cancelled, and then the order will remain registered in the High Court only. If the registration in the High Court is cancelled, the re-registration in the magistrates' court automatically ceases. Upon cancellation of the re-registration, the justices' clerk is required to notify both the High Court and the court of origin in Scotland or Northern Ireland. Just as a justices' clerk is required to enter particulars of registrations, and cancellations thereof, in his court register and to notify the courts and parties concerned in cases of direct registrations from Scotland and Northern Ireland (see para 11 and 12) he must also cause entries of re-registrations, and cancellations thereof, to be similarly made and the like notices to be sent to the respondent and complainant.

The Magistrates' Courts (Maintenance Orders Act 1958) (Amendment) Rules 1980 sets up the machinery for the operation of the scheme and prescribed forms are set out in the schedule to those rules.

However, there is one important difference between a directly registered summary court order and an order of the Scottish Court of Session or the Northern Irish High Court which has been re-registered via the English High Court. It concerns the variation and discharge of such orders. The magistrates' court in which the order is re-registered has no power to vary or discharge an order of the Court of Session or the Northern Irish High Court. Orders of courts of summary jurisdiction in Scotland and Northern Ireland registered in magistrates' courts may be varied as to the rate of payments (but not otherwise) — (see para. 13 hereof). Where, however, an application to vary or discharge a re-registered Scottish or Northern Irish High Court order is received, an ex parte hearing should be arranged before the justices, when the evidence in support of the application should be taken by way of signed and sworn deposition, and then transmitted with the complaint to the Court of Session or High Court of Northern Ireland, by the justices' clerk, for final determination.

Orders of Scottish and Northern Irish courts of summary jurisdiction registered in magistrates' courts in England and Wales may also be re-registered in the English High Court under the Maintenance Orders Act 1958. In this event, the magistrates' court will continue to have power to vary the order as to rate of payments, but will lose its power to enforce it. Notice of the variation must be given to the English High Court as well as to the Court of origin.

Complete guidance as to the operation of the scheme is to be found in Home Office circ. 124/1980.

11   **Certified Copies of Orders Received from Scotland and Northern Ireland for Registration and Enforcement in Magistrates' Courts.**

The justices' clerk must, upon receiving the certified copy of such an order, cause the same to be entered in his court register, by means of a memorandum. The memorandum must be signed by the justices' clerk. The memorandum should state that the order is registered in the particular court served by the justices' clerk and should contain the date of registration. The justices' clerk then has a duty to notify the clerk of the original court that the order has been registered. Notice of registration must also be sent to the respondent by recorded delivery or registered post. The notice should state that payments under the order have now become payable through the said justices' clerk. It is good practice to notify the complainant that registration has been effected, and advise her as to the methods open to her for enforcement. The order, once registered, becomes for enforcement purposes, an order of the registering court, and the clerk may proceed in his own name for the recovery of the arrears as though the order were an affiliation order.

12. **Cancellation of Registration**

The registration of an order shall be cancelled if:

1. An application is made by or on behalf of the person entitled to payments under the order, for the cancellation of the registration (but not if variation proceedings are pending in the court of registration)

2. Notice is received from the original court that the respondent is no longer resident in the country of registration. (Maintenance Orders Act 1950, s.24)

Application under para. (1) above for the cancellation of registration in an English or Welsh court of a Scottish or Northern Irish order shall be made to the clerk of the registering court by lodging a written application and a copy of the order which is so registered. The application shall state the date of registration. Where the justices' clerk cancels the registration, he shall notify the clerk of the original court of that fact.

Where an order has been made in England or Wales, and that order has been registered in Scotland or Northern Ireland, and the person liable to make the payments under the order has ceased to reside in the country of registration, that person may make an application either orally or in writing, to a justice of the court which made the order, for cancellation of the registration. If he does not appear in person he must file a statutory declaration with the justices' clerk for that court stating the facts in support of the application. If the justice is satisfied that the applicant has ceased to reside in the country of registration, he shall cause the justices' clerk to send notice to that effect to the court of registration. The registration will then be cancelled by the clerk of the registering court, and notice will be sent to the justices' clerk who must enter particulars of such notice of cancellation in his court register.

Where the registration of an order is cancelled, notice of the cancellation must be sent by registered or recorded delivery post to the person liable to make the payments under the order. However, any payment in accordance with the directions made upon registration of the order shall be deemed to have been properly made under the order until such time as the payer receives notice of the cancellation.

Where a provision in an English or Welsh order requiring payments to be made through an English or Welsh justices' clerk has ceased to have effect upon registration in Scotland or Northern Ireland, that provision is deemed to be restored to the order upon cancellation of registration.

13. **Discharge and Variation of Registered Orders.**
    Maintenance Orders Act 1950. s.22.
    Where a maintenance order is for the time being registered under Part II of the Act of 1950 in a court of summary jurisdiction, or a sheriff court, that court may, upon application being made by or on behalf of the person liable to make the payments, or the person entitled to those payments, *vary the order as to the rate of payments*. However, no variation of payments shall be such as to increase the amount above the maximum, if any, authorized by the law of the part of the United Kingdom where the order was originally made. Courts in England and Wales are, therefore, authorized to take judicial notice of the law of Scotland and Northern Ireland regarding the maximum amount, if any, payable under the orders made in those countries. A summons upon a complaint for the variation of an order is to be served in the same manner as that for proceedings leading to original orders. (paragraphs 2,3 and 4 hereof.)

    It should be noted that registered orders may only be varied by the court of registration in so far as it affects the rate of payment. If application is to be made for the discharge of the order, or any other type of variation apart from the rate of payment, the application must be determined by the original court. (But see para.10 of this Guide in so far as it affects variations of re-registered High Court orders).

    Where a maintenance order is for the time being registered under Part II of the 1950 Act, either the payer or the payee may make application to the original court, or court of registration, as the case may be, to adduce evidence in support of an application to vary or discharge the order. The court in which the evidence is adduced shall cause the evidence to be written down and signed by the deponent, and to be forwarded to the clerk of the registering court, or original court, as the case may be. This evidence, once taken, sworn and signed, shall be evidence of the facts stated therein. It should be noted that depositions of this nature, although admissible as evidence, are not conclusive evidence of the facts stated therein. The facts stated therein can be challenged by the other party. Therefore, there is no reason why the court dealing with an application should not, if it thinks it desirable in the interests of justice, remit the matter to the court where the evidence was taken with a request that further evidence relating to specific points raised by the other party, if necessary, be taken from the deponent.

    Where an order from Scotland or Northern Ireland is registered in England or Wales, and the payer requires, for example, a reduction in the order, his complaint is lodged, and a summons for variation is drawn up and transmitted to the Scottish or Northern Irish court for endorsement and subsequent service. Sworn evidence taken from the respondent, and any witnesses, in Scotland or Northern Ireland, and transmitted to the registering court would, therefore, be admissible in whole, or as part of, the defence in the proceedings upon the hearing of the complaint. However, where the payer desires to apply for the discharge of the order, or, e.g. to delete a provision for a child's maintenance, it is suggested that his complaint be drawn up, an ex-parte hearing arranged, the sworn evidence taken by way of deposition, and the complaint and sworn deposition be then transmitted to the clerk of the original court for determination.

    Section 23 of the Act of 1950 provides that where an Order which has been registered under Part II is varied by the registering court, notice of the variation shall be sent to the original court, and such notice shall be registered by the clerk of the original court. If the order is varied or discharged by any other court, notice of the fact shall be sent to the court of registration and the Clerk of the Court shall record the notice in his register.

Under r.4(2) of the Maintenance Orders Act 1950 (Summary Jurisdiction) Rules 1950 where the discharge or variation of an English or Welsh order registered in Scotland or Northern Ireland has taken place, the justices' clerk shall send a certified copy of the variation order, or order of revocation, as the case may be, to the clerk of the original court.

14. **Transfer of Wife Maintenance Proceedings.**

A defendant residing in Scotland or Northern Ireland who has received a summons to appear before a court in England or Wales, may apply to that court for the proceedings to be removed into another court in England or Wales, being a court area where the parties last ordinarily resided as man and wife. The application may be dealt with by a single justice. The justice hearing the application must afford the wife an opportunity of being heard, unless he decides to refuse the application forthwith. Where the application is granted, the clerk of the original court shall send the complaint, summons and any other relevant documents to the court where the parties last ordinarily resided as man and wife and the matter shall then be deemed to have been commenced in that Court. (Rule 1 of the 1950 Rules).

15. **RECIPROCAL ENFORCEMENT IN COMMONWEALTH COUNTRIES**

Reciprocal enforcement in the countries of the Commonwealth may, generally speaking, be divided into two parts:

First, reciprocal arrangements under the Maintenance Orders (Facilities for Enforcement) Act 1920, and

Secondly, reciprocal arrangements under the Maintenance Orders (Reciprocal Enforcement) Act 1972.

The Act of 1920 is effectively repealed by s.22 of the Act of 1972, but remains in force in so far as it relates to reciprocal arrangements with countries and territories not yet designated by Order in Council as a reciprocating country under the Act of 1972. The various Orders in Council provide, and will continue to provide, transitional provisions for orders registered and confirmed under the 1920 Act to be re-registered under the 1972 Act to preserve the continuity of the existing 1920 Act orders.

16. **The Maintenance Orders (Facilities for Enforcement) Act 1920.**
Countries to Which Extended.

On the whole, this Act has worked satisfactorily, but it has its limitations. At present, it applies to the countries set out in Appendix "A" to this Guide.

17. **Application of Act to Maintenance Orders Only.**

This Act applies only to "Maintenance Orders" for the periodical payment of sums of money towards the maintenance of the wife or other dependants of the person against whom the order is made. "Dependants" means such persons as that person is, according to the law in force in the part of the Commonwealth in which the order is made, liable to maintain.

18. **Affiliation Orders.**
    The Act specifically excludes affiliation orders.

19. **Transmission by Overseas Court of Substantive Order for Registration in England or Wales.**
    Section 1 of the Act, and the Maintenance Orders (Facilities for Enforcement) Rules 1922 provide that where a maintenance order has been made in any of the countries or territories outside the United Kingdom, to which the Act extends, and a certified copy thereof has been transmitted to the Secretary of State, the Secretary of State shall send a copy of the order to the appropriate justices' clerk for the area where the defendant is alleged to reside. On receipt of the order, the justices' clerk shall register the order in his court register, in such manner as to show it is registered under the 1920 Act, thus distinguishing it from other entries. When the order has been registered, the court shall, unless it is undesirable to do so, direct that payments be made through the justices' clerk, or such other person as may be specified. Upon registration, the order becomes as if it were an order of the registering court, and that court shall have power to enforce it accordingly.

20. **Function of Justices' Clerk.**
    The justices' clerk has power to proceed in his own name for the recovery of the arrears.

21. **Variation etc., of Orders Registered Under s.1 and Cancellation of Registration.**
    It should be noted, however, that there is no power to vary or discharge an order registered under s.1 of the 1920 Act. There would appear to be no specific provision in the Act, or Rules made thereunder, in regard to cancellation of registration.

22. **Overseas Superior Court Orders to be Registered in the English High Court.**
    Orders made by Superior Courts overseas must be registered in the High Court.

23. **Transmission Overseas of Substantive Order Made by English or Welsh Court for Registration and Enforcement.**
    Section 2 of the Act provides the machinery whereby a maintenance order made by a court in England or Wales may be transmitted to a reciprocating country abroad, being a country to which the Act extends, for enforcement.
    This section presupposes that a substantive order is in force, and that the payer under the order has, since the order was made, gone to reside in one of the reciprocating countries. In this event, where the court is satisfied that the payer is residing in a country to which this Act extends, the justices' clerk shall send to the Secretary of State, for transmission to the Governor of the overseas territory, a certified copy of the order.
    It is helpful for the following documents, also, to be sent, namely:
    1. A sworn statement of the arrears, if any,
    2. A photograph of the defendant,
    3. A statement sufficient to establish the whereabouts of the payer,
    4. The name and address of the justices' clerk to whom payments should

be sent by the overseas registering court.

Once the order is registered overseas, communications between the respective clerks can take place direct, rather than through the Home Office.

For transmission of county court orders under this section, application should be made to the registrar of the county court.

There would appear to be no power to vary an order registered under this section by increasing the payments unless both parties are either present or legally represented.

24. **Jurisdiction of Magistrates' Court to Make a Provisional Order Against a Person Residing in a Reciprocating Country.**

Section 3 provides the machinery under which a Court in England and Wales is empowered to make a maintenance order where the complainant is residing in England or Wales and the defendant is residing in a reciprocating country to which the Act extends, and therefore cannot be served with a summons. Proceedings with a view to obtaining affiliation orders are excluded by the Act. The proceedings before the magistrates' courts in England and Wales are ex parte; such proceedings are domestic proceedings for the purposes of the Magistrates' Courts Act 1980. The evidence given by the complainant and her witnesses, if any, is put into writing in the same manner as a witness who is giving oral evidence before examining justices. After each witness, including the complainant, has completed his or her evidence, the evidence is read back to the witness and signed by him or her. It is good practice for the adjudicating justices to sign a jurat at the foot of each completed deposition underneath the witness' signature to the effect that such deposition was taken and sworn before them at........Magistrates' Court on the.......day of.......19... It is also recommended that the witness initials each page of the deposition. It has also been found convenient to include in the deposition of the complainant, preferably at the commencement of her evidence, the full name and address of her husband and a personal description of him. Where a photograph is available, this should be produced and made an exhibit. An essential exhibit is the marriage certificate, as the marriage has to be strictly proved. Where maintenance is being sought for children of the family, a birth certificate of each child is also an essential exhibit. If the court is satisfied that the ground of the complaint has been made out, it is empowered to make a maintenance order against the husband. However, the order must be expressed as being provisional only, and to be of no effect unless and until it is confirmed by a competent court in the country or territory where the husband is residing.

Some doubt exists as to whether a magistrates' court has power to make a custody order, but in cases under the Guardianship of Minors Act 1971, for example, unless a custody clause is contained in the order, there would be no power to include maintenance provision for the child. Compare, however, with s.3(3) of the 1972 Act — para.40.

After the provisional order has been made, a certified copy of the order must be sent to the Secretary of State together with the depositions, a list of the exhibits, the actual exhibits specified in the list, and also a statement of the grounds upon which the making of the order might have been opposed by the husband had he been served with a summons and had appeared at the hearing. This statement should be drawn up with great care. (See form 4). It must set out all the grounds of defence open to the defendant under the Law of England and Wales. The statement should be signed by one of the justices adjudicating, or the justices' clerk. The reason for this is that the court overseas will determine the matter under the law of England and Wales, although, of course, it will adopt its own local procedure in dealing with the matter.

25. **Remission by Overseas Court for Taking of Further Evidence.**

If the overseas court requires further evidence, it will remit the matter back to the original court with a request for further evidence to be taken. Usually, a transcript of the evidence taken in the overseas court accompanies the request. Sometimes, the request will contain a specific demand that a particular witness be examined. More often, it is the complainant herself whose further evidence will be required, usually in order to refute or confirm some fact of facts alleged by or on behalf of the defendant in the court overseas. Sometimes, the overseas court will set out specifically the matters upon which the complainant or witness is to be examined, or further examined. The further evidence must be taken and recorded in exactly the same way as the evidence taken in the original proceedings, that is, by way of signed and sworn deposition. It must then be forwarded to the Secretary of State for transmission overseas. The further evidence may be taken by the original court or by any court acting for the same Commission Area as the original court. Notice of the fact that the overseas court requires further evidence must be served upon the complainant. The notice shall state the nature of the further evidence required and the date appointed for the taking thereof. If necessary, a witness summons may issue to compel attendance of any witness who is to be examined.

26. **Power to Rescind Provisional Order Following Taking of Further Evidence.**

If, after taking the further evidence, the Court in England or Wales is of opinion that the provisional order should not have been made, the court may rescind the provisional order, and that is the end of the matter. Although there is nothing in the Act or the Rules made thereunder requiring the clerk to do so, it is good practice to inform the Secretary of State and the overseas court that, after the taking of further evidence, the court has seen fit to rescind the provisional order.

27. **Appeals**

A right of appeal exists against the refusal of the court to make a provisional order. This right is deemed to be conferred by s.29 of the Domestic Proceedings and Magistrates' Courts Act 1978.

28. **Notification of Confirmation of Order and Subsequent Correspondence Between Courts.**

The overseas court will, in due course, notify the justices' clerk of the fact that the matter has come before that court. Usually, this takes the form of a letter from the clerk of the overseas court enclosing a certified copy of the confirmation order, or certificate of non-confirmation, as the case may be. Formal notice is also received from the Secretary of State. If the order is confirmed, the overseas court will undertake enforcement, and correspondence regarding enforcement should be conducted direct between courts, rather than through the Secretary of State.

29. **Variation and Revocation of Provisional Order Which has Been Confirmed.**

Where a provisional maintenance order made by a magistrates' court in England or Wales has been confirmed by an overseas court, the order may be varied or rescinded by a magistrates' court in England or Wales, and on the making of such an order, a certified copy thereof must be sent to the Secretary of State for transmission, through the usual diplomatic channels, to the overseas court which has confirmed the order. The order may be rescinded upon the application of the wife, and the proceedings contemplated are ex parte. See next paragraph hereof (para. 30) where the variation sought is an increase in the amount of the payments.

30. **Power to make provisional order increasing payments under an order which has been confirmed overseas.**

Where, however, the complainant seeks to vary the order by providing for an increase in the payments thereunder, and the magistrates' court thinks it proper to increase the amount of the order, such variation order is to be provisional only, and cannot have effect unless and until it is confirmed by the overseas court. In variation proceedings of this nature, the evidence should be taken by way of sworn deposition, in the same way as at the original hearing, and transmitted to the Secretary of State with the provisional variation order.

31. **Jurisdiction of English and Welsh courts to confirm provisional maintenance order made overseas.**

This power is contained in s.4 of the Maintenance Orders (Facilities for Enforcement) Act 1920.

Where a provisional order of maintenance has been made in an overseas court and transmitted to the court in England or Wales having jurisdiction where the respondent resides, by the Secretary of State, that court has power to confirm the order, either with or without modification. The provisional order will be accompanied by the depositions of the witnesses, the exhibits, if any, and also a statement of the grounds upon which, under the appropriate Dominion Court Law, the respondent could have contested the proceedings had he been served with a summons and had been present at the hearing. In sending the documents to the appropriate justices' clerk, the Secretary of State will request that the justices issue a summons to the respondent. The summons, and service thereof, is to be treated as if it were a summons of the issuing court, as, indeed, it is.

It is as well to mention at this juncture that the Magistrates' Courts Act 1980 shall apply to all such proceedings before magistrates' courts; the depositions taken overseas are admissible in evidence to the same extent as oral evidence of the facts would be admissible, and that any signature on the documents purporting to be that of a judicial officer overseas shall be deemed to be such unless the contrary is proved.

The summons issued to the respondent should recite the terms of the provisional order, and should call upon the respondent to appear before the magistrates' court to show cause why the order should not be confirmed. (Form 1).

Neither the Act, nor the rules, require that the statement of grounds of defence open to the respondent under the Dominion Law should be served upon the respondent; it is nevertheless good practice to attach a copy of the statement to the summons, as this will often be of assistance to the respondent's solicitor, who may not be familiar with the Dominion Law under which the provisional order was made. It is also good practice to add a foot-note to the summons indicating that a copy of the depositions taken overseas in support of the provisional order will be supplied on request. It goes without saying that this information will be of assistance to the solicitor for the respondent in taking instructions and advising his client as to whether or not he should oppose the confirmation, or make submissions for confirmation with modification or alteration.

At the hearing it is open to the respondent to raise any defence which he could have raised under the appropriate Dominion Law, but no other defence. If it transpires that a particular defence is open to the respondent under the Dominion Law, but that ground is not one of the grounds set out in the statement supplied to the court, this will not preclude the respondent from raising that defence, but such occasions are rare. Having said this, the statement supplied by the Dominion court setting out the grounds upon which objection may be taken shall be taken as conclusive evidence that each ground set out therein is a good defence under the Dominion Law.

The proceedings should be commenced by the clerk reading to the justices the evidence which has been transmitted from overseas, and drawing to the justices' attention the fact that a provisional order has been made, and the terms of such order.

The respondent should then be called upon to show cause why the order should not be confirmed. If he, through his legal representative (if he has one) consents to the confirmation, the order is confirmed accordingly and his consent is entered in the court register. If he fails to appear, and proof exists that he has had the summons, again there is no reason before the court why the order should not be confirmed.

In the above two situations mentioned, the only modification which would appear to be necessary is the conversion of the maintenance payments expressed in the provisional order from the overseas currency to the equivalent amount in British sterling at the rate of exchange prevailing on the day when the order is confirmed.

If the respondent appears and contends that the order should not be confirmed, and in support thereof, raises any of the defences open to him under the appropriate Dominion Law, it is advisable to take his evidence, and that of his witnesses (if any) in the form of a deposition, which should then be signed by each deponent, and attested by the justices. The reason for this is that if, after hearing the evidence adduced, the court is satisfied that for the purpose of any defence raised, it is necessary to remit the case to the original court overseas for the taking of further evidence, the depositions so taken, or a certified copy thereof, can be sent to the Secretary of State with the order of remission. The order, where appropriate, should specify the nature of the further evidence required. Sometimes, the further evidence required will be simply the complainant's or witness' answer to allegations made by the respondent in his evidence. On other occasions, it may be a request for a particular person, who has not already been called, to be examined. The hearing will then be adjourned until the further evidence has been received by the justices' clerk from the overseas court.

After all the evidence has been heard by the magistrates' court, whether upon the first hearing, or, at the adjourned hearing (if the case was remitted for further evidence) the court will decide whether or not the complaint has been proved. If the court decides that the complaint has been proved it will confirm the provisional order in principle subject to any modifications to be determined; otherwise it will refuse to confirm the order. If the order is thus confirmed, the court will then determine what modification, if any, should be made to the order. Generally, such modification will take the form of adjusting the maintenance payments in accordance with the means of the respondent and ordering the payments to be made in sterling. Payments must be ordered to be made through the justices' clerk, unless there is good reason for ordering otherwise.

A certified copy of the order of confirmation must be sent to the Secretary of State, or where the order has not been confirmed, notice of that fact should be sent to the Secretary of State. A certified copy of the confirmation order (or non-confirmation as the case may be) must also be sent direct to the overseas court.

As with a registered order under this Act, it becomes the duty of the justices' clerk to enforce the order.

It should be noted that by s.6 of the Act, every order registered or confirmed under the Act is enforceable as a civil debt *unless* the order is one which, if made in England and Wales, could be enforced as an affiliation order, e.g., wife maintenance orders and Guardianship of Minors Orders. A warrant of distress, or warrant of commitment in respect of arrears due under such an order can be executed anywhere in the United Kingdom.

It should be noted that, in deciding whether or not the provisional order should be confirmed, the magistrates' court will be applying the law of the Dominion concerned, but the procedure in the court itself will, of course, be in accordance with the law of England and Wales.

32. **Right of Appeal of Respondent.**

The respondent has the same right of appeal against the confirmation of an order as he would have if an order had been made against him under the Domestic Proceedings and Magistrates' Courts Act 1978.

33. **Power of court to vary a provisional order which has been confirmed.**

Section 4(6) of the 1920 Act provides that a provisional order so confirmed may be varied or rescinded in the like manner as if it had been originally made in the confirming court, and that the court upon such application, may remit the case to the original court for the purpose of taking any further evidence as it deems necessary. In the case of such an application, it would seem that for the interests of justice to be served, the applicant's (or payer's) evidence should be taken by way of deposition and a certified copy thereof, together with the complaint, be transmitted to the Secretary of State with a request that the wife's (or payee's) evidence in reply thereto be taken before the overseas court, and any witnesses she may wish to call, and once this further evidence is received, the confirming court will be in possession of all the facts to enable it to make a proper adjudication on the question of variation or recission.

34. **Admissibility of depositions taken overseas.**

Depositions adduced in evidence in proceedings under this Act are admissible in the same way as oral evidence of those facts would admissible. The facts contained in the depositions are not conclusive evidence of those facts. Therefore, once the court has heard all the evidence, both by way of deposition and oral evidence, it is entitled to come to a conclusion as to where the truth lies. The justices may prefer the evidence contained in the depositions to that of the husband's oral evidence, or vice versa, and find accordingly.

Here lies one of the difficulties, as experienced justices are very often able to judge by a person's reaction in the witness box as to whether he is speaking the truth, but sworn evidence written on a piece of paper is another matter.

THE MAINTENANCE ORDERS (RECIPROCAL ENFORCEMENT) ACT 1972 — PART I. RECIPROCATING COUNTRIES

35. **Designation of "reciprocating" and "convention" countries.**
The reciprocal provisions of this Act are contained in two Parts. Part I deals with the reciprocal arrangements with, broadly speaking, the Commonwealth countries, the Hague Convention countries and the Republic of Ireland. Part II deals with reciprocal arrangements with the E.E.C and foreign countries. The countries designated under Part I are set out in Appendix "B" hereto, and are known as "Reciprocating Countries". Appendix "C" hereto sets out the countries designated under Part 11 of the Act and are known as "Convention Countries". Special provisions exist under a modified Part I in relation to the Irish Republic and the Hague Convention countries. Therefore, the reciprocal provisions in relation to the Irish Republic and the Hague Convention Countries are dealt with under separate headings.

36. **Reciprocating Countries — Part I of the Act of 1972.**
This part of the Act applies to maintenance orders generally. However, some of the countries designated, by reason of their domestic legislation, exclude certain types of orders. These exclusions have been noted in Appendix "B" opposite the name of the country concerned. The machinery providing for the operation of Part I is governed by the Magistrates' Courts (Reciprocal Enforcement of Maintenance Orders) Rules 1974 (hereinafter called the "1974 rules".)

37. **Outward transmission of substantive order.**
Section 2 of the Act deals with the situation where, after a maintenance order has been made by a court in the United Kingdom, the payer moves to reside in a reciprocating country. The payee has a right under the said s.2 to apply *to the prescribed officer of the court which made the order* for the order to be sent to the reciprocating country for enforcement. Under the 1974 Rules the prescribed officer, in so far as a magistrates' court is concerned, is the justices' clerk. The application may be made in writing, and if it is made in writing, shall include the following details:
(1) the date the order was made,
(2) the payer's address,
(3) matters likely to assist in the identification of the payer,
(4) a photograph of the payer, if one is available.
Upon application being received by the justices' clerk, the latter must, if he is satisfied that the payer is residing in a reciprocating country, send the following documents to the Secretary of State, with a view to their being sent to the appropriate authority in the reciprocating country;

1. a certified copy of the maintenance order,
2. a certificate signed by the justices' clerk that the order is enforceable in the United Kingdom,
3. a certificate of arrears, so signed,
4. a statement giving such information that the justices' clerk possesses as to the whereabouts of the payer,
5. a statement giving such information as the justices' clerk possesses for facilitating the identification of the payer,
6. where available, a photograph of the payer.

The above procedure does not apply to provisional orders, or to orders made under Part II of the Act (Convention Orders). The registration of the order in a reciprocating country does not affect any jurisdiction with respect to it of a court in the United Kingdom, and such order may be enforced, varied or revoked by a United Kingdom court. (Section 2 (5) of the Act of 1972) This subsection would appear to remove any doubts about enforcement should the payer return to the United Kingdom while the order is still registered overseas, or any powers of the High Court with regard to the order.

After notice of registration of the order has been received from the overseas court, communications concerning enforcement etc., will normally take place direct between the clerks of the courts concerned.

38 Difference between orders registered overseas under 1920 Act and 1972 Act.

The difference between orders registered overseas under s.2 of the Maintenance Orders (Reciprocal Enforcement) Act 1972 and s.2 of the Maintenance Orders (Facilities for Enforcement) Act 1920 is that, under the Act of 1972, registered orders can be varied by the United Kingdom court. The variation of such orders is made possible by s.5 of the Act of 1972, and is fully dealt with under the heading "Variation and Revocation of Maintenance Orders made in England and Wales" (para. 49).

39. Jurisdiction of magistrates' courts to make provisional order against person residing outside the United Kingdom.

Section 3 of the Maintenance Orders (Reciprocal Enforcement) Act 1972 confers upon courts in the United Kingdom power to make provisional maintenance orders against persons residing in countries designated as reciprocating countries. Appendix "B" hereto gives a list of such countries. A complaint for a maintenance order against a person residing in a reciprocating country must be lodged with the justices' clerk, who will arrange an ex parte hearing before the appropriate domestic court in his area. The complaint is made under the statute under which the required relief is sought, e.g., the Domestic Proceedings and Magistrates' Courts Act 1978, the Guardianship of Minors Act 1971, and so on; therefore, jurisdiction to hear the complaint is in accordance with the original enabling statute, the Magistrates' Courts Act 1980, and the above cited Act of 1972. But where a respondent is residing in a reciprocating country, it is not possible to serve a summons on him. The court can only, therefore, hear the evidence of the complainant and her witnesses. If, after hearing the evidence, the court is of opinion that the complaint has been made out, it may make an order for the maintenance of the complainant and any children of the family. Since the respondent has not been served with a summons or notice of proceedings, s.3 provides that an order made in these circumstances shall be a provisional order only.

40. **Power to make maintenance order for child without first determining question of custody.**

In proceedings where the magistrates' court does not have the power to make a maintenance order for a child unless the legal custody of the child has already been determined, if the court is satisfied that there are grounds disclosed by the evidence justifying the making of such a maintenance order, then, in order for the court to make the order, the complainant shall be deemed to be the person to whom the legal custody of the child has been committed by an order of the court. (Section 3(3) of the Act of 1972)

41. **No power to refuse order on grounds that matter is more suitable for the High Court.**

By s.3(3) of the Act of 1972, where a complaint is being dealt with under s.3 the magistrates' court is not empowered to refuse to make an order on the grounds that the matter ought to be dealt with by the High Court.

42. **Procedure to be followed upon application for provisional order.**

The evidence of the complainant and her witnesses is to be taken in deposition form in the same manner as that described in the section of this Guide relating to the procedure under s.3 of the Act of 1920. See para. 24.

43. **The making of the provisional order and the amount thereof.**

If the court is satisfied, upon the evidence, that the complaint is made out, it will make a provisional order of maintenance. Often, there will be no evidence as to the respondent's means so that the amount determined by the justices to be payable under the order will be pure guess work. The court in the reciprocating country, if it confirms the order in principle, will be able to modify the provisional order in so far as it concerns the amount payable thereunder, so that it is in line with the respondent's means.

44. **Procedure to be followed by justices' clerk following the making of the provisional order.**

After the court has made a provisional order, the justices' clerk must send the following documents to the Secretary of State:-
    1. a certified copy of the provisional order (form 3)
    2. the sworn depositions taken in support of the complaint,
    3. a certificate signed by the justices' clerk certifying that the grounds stated in the certificate are the grounds on which the making of the order might have been opposed by the payer under the order (form 4)
    4. a statement giving such information as was available to the court as to the whereabouts of the payer,
    5. a statement giving such information as the justices' clerk possesses for facilitating the identification of the payer,
    6. where available, a photograph of the payer.

It is often convenient to include the information required in Nos. 4 and 5 above in the first part of the complainant's sworn deposition. Where the application is for an order under ss.2,6, or 7 of the Domestic Proceedings and Magistrates' Courts Act 1978 the marriage must be strictly proved. The marriage certificate will, therefore, be produced as an exhibit. Similarly, where maintenance is being sought in respect of a child, the birth certificate must be produced. It may also be convenient to include the photograph, where available, as an exhibit. All other documents produced in support of the complainant's case should also be made exhibits. A list of the exhibits should be drawn up, and the original exhibits, together with a list thereof, transmitted to the Secretary of State with the sworn depositions, provisional order and the other documents required by the Act.

The file of documents sent to the Secretary of State should be accompanied by a letter requesting that the case be transmitted to the reciprocating country with a view to the provisional order being confirmed and enforced. (s.3(5) of the Act of 1972)

45. **Remission by overseas court for taking of further evidence.**

It may be that, before determining the matter, the court in the reciprocating country will require further evidence to be taken either from the witnesses who have already given evidence in support of the provisional order, or from witnesses whom the respondent wishes to be examined. If this is so, the case will be remitted to the original court, with such a request. The justices' clerk will serve notice of such request upon the person or persons to be examined or re-examined and, if necessary, issue a witness summons to compel attendance. The appropriate witness expenses may be paid to any person so required to appear, unless he or she happens to be the complainant (or the respondent) (s.14 of the Act of 1972). In most cases, upon the case being remitted for further evidence a copy of the evidence already taken in the reciprocating country will accompany the order of remission.

The Magistrates' Courts (Reciprocal Enforcement of Maintenance Orders) Rules 1974, r.10, provides that the evidence will be taken by the court making the order or such court as the Secretary of State requests. Arrangments may be made, if necessary, for the evidence to be taken by another magistrates' court if the witness happens to reside in the area of that other court.

If the overseas court requests that the evidence be taken in a particular manner, the magistrates' court to which the case is remitted shall, so far as is practicable, comply with that request, but subject to this, the evidence must be taken in the form of a signed and sworn deposition, and must be attested by the justices. In other words, in the same manner as the evidence given in the original proceedings. In some cases, the further evidence is to be sent to the Secretary of State for transmission abroad. In other cases, the evidence is to be forwarded direct to the overseas court. The method of transmitting the evidence so taken in response to a request from a reciprocating court is indicated in the appropriate column of Appendix "B" hereto.

46. **Revocation of provisional order following remission from overseas and the taking of the further evidence.**

There may be occasions when the magistrates' court which has made the provisional order will

(1) upon receiving from overseas the evidence given by or on behalf of the respondent, and

(2) upon taking the further evidence required by the overseas court,

consider that the provisional order should not have been made in the first place. As a result, it may wish to revoke the order. The court has power to do this. However, before doing so, it must send a notice to the complainant setting out:

(1) the evidence received from the overseas court and the further evidence taken in response to the overseas court's request,

(2) inform the complainant that it appears to the court that the provisional maintenance order ought not to have been made, and

(3) (a) Inform the complainant that if she wishes to make representations with respect to the evidence set out in the notice, she may do so orally or in writing;

(b) that if the complainant so wishes, she may adduce further evidence, and

(c) if it is her wish to adduce further evidence to inform the justices' clerk accordingly.

If the complainant informs the justices' clerk that further evidence is to be adduced, the justices' clerk must notify the complainant of the date fixed for the taking of such evidence.

In practical terms the case will already have been adjourned by the justices after they considered revoking the order, so that the notice can be served. Therefore, the adjourned hearing can be used not only for taking of any further evidence which the complainant wishes to adduce, but also for the consideration by the justices of any oral or written representations by the complainant, or, more probably, by her legal representative. The justices, after hearing the representations, will then either revoke the order or re-transmit the case overseas, so that the overseas court can finally determine the issue of confirmation or non-confirmation of the order. (Maintenance Orders (Reciprocal Enforcement) Act 1972, Section 5(9) and r.7 of the Magistrates' Courts (Reciprocal Enforcement of Maintenance Orders) Rules 1974).

47. **Effect of confirmation of provisional order.**

By s.3(6) of the Act of 1972, where a provisional order has been confirmed overseas, it then becomes an order of the original magistrates' court for all purposes, as if the magistrates' court had made it in the form in which it was confirmed. Such order may be revoked, varied and enforced as though it were an order of the English or Welsh magistrates' court. Therefore, if the respondent were to return to the United Kingdom, the order could be enforced here or could be registered under s.2 of the Act of 1972 were the respondent to remove to another reciprocating country.

48. **Enforcement of Confirmed Order Overseas.**

While the respondent remains resident in the reciprocating country, where the order was confirmed, the confirming court will attend to all enforcement procedures, and correspondence between the original magistrates' court and the confirming court relating to enforcement can be conducted direct between the respective clerks.

49. **Variation and revocation of maintenance orders made in England and Wales — s.5 of the Act of 1972.**

Where a substantive order made in England or Wales has been registered in a reciprocating country, or where a provisional order has been made and has been duly confirmed by a court in a reciprocating country, the court in England and Wales is given power to vary that order.

However, unless either:

(1) both parties to the order appear in the proceedings, or

(2) the applicant appears, but the respondent, having been duly served with the appropriate process, does not,

any variation of the order by way of an increase in the payments shall be provisional only. "Appropriate process" means, in England and Wales, a summons issued and served in accordance with the Magistrates' Courts Act 1980 and rules; if service is to be effected in Scotland or Northern Ireland, that summons duly endorsed in accordance with s.15 of the Maintenance Orders Act 1950 (see para.3 ante).

This provision would appear to provide for the situation where both parties are living once again in the United Kingdom. However, where one of the parties still happens to be in a reciprocating country, it is not possible to serve him with process, therefore, the Act provides that any upward variation of the order can only be provisional.

Where proceedings leading to the making of a provisional variation order are contemplated, the evidence must be taken in deposition form, and the depositions are to be transmitted by the justices' clerk, with a certified copy of the provisional order of variation, to the reciprocating court. The depositions must be authenticated by one of the justices before whom it is taken, stating that it is the original document, or a true copy of that document. Exhibits should be similarly authenticated. The deposition must be read over to the witness and be signed by the witness.

In some cases, the provisional order of variation and supporting documents may be sent direct to the reciprocating court; in others, the documents are to be sent via the Home Office. The appropriate course is indicated in Appendix "B" hereto.

Under s.5(5) of the Act of 1972, where a certified copy of a provisional order made by a court in a reciprocating country, which is an order varying or revoking an order made in England or Wales and registered in a reciprocating country, or is an order varying or revoking an order confirmed by a court in a reciprocating country, is received by the court in England or Wales which originally made the order, and the provisional order is accompanied by a duly authenticated document setting out the evidence given in the proceedings in support of the provisional variation or revocation order the Court may confirm or refuse to confirm the provisional order as the case may be. If the order is a provisional variation order, the court in England or Wales may confirm it without alteration, or with such alteration as it thinks fit. The magistrates' court, for the purpose of determining whether the provisional order should be confirmed is required to proceed as if the application for variation or revocation had been made to it. Therefore, the evidence transmitted from the reciprocating country can be regarded as the complaint, and a summons issued in consequence thereof to the party against whom the provisional revocation or variation order was made. It is good practice to recite in the summons the terms of the provisional order and the summons should contain a direction to the person summoned to appear to show cause why the provisional order should not be confirmed, with or without such alteration as the court thinks fit. A copy of the evidence transmitted by the overseas court with the provisional order should be attached to the summons. At this juncture, it should be borne in mind that if the court in England or Wales which is determining the issue of whether or not to confirm a provisional order desires further evidence from overseas for the purpose of the proceedings, it has power under s.14(5) of the Act of 1972 to request the overseas court to take further evidence on such matters as may be specified in the request. If the magistrates' court makes this request, a copy of the evidence taken so far in the "confirmation" proceedings should be annexed to the request. Under r.11 of the 1974 Rules, the magistrates' court's request for any additional evidence is to be communicated in writing direct to the court in question.

Where an order is varied or revoked under s.5, written notice must be sent to the Secretary of State, and to the court in which the order is registered or confirmed.

50. **Registration in England and Wales of orders made in reciprocating countries — s.6 of the Act of 1972.**

This section authorises a court in the United Kingdom to register an order (not being a provisional order) which has been made in a reciprocating country. The order is forwarded by the Secretary of State to, in England and Wales, the justices' clerk for the area where the payer under the order is residing. Upon receipt of the order, the justices' clerk shall take such steps as he thinks fit to ascertain if the payer is residing within the jurisdiction of the court. If it transpires that the payer is not within his jurisdiction, he must return the order to the Home Office with such information as he possesses as to the whereabouts of the payer. If the payer is residing within the jurisdiction of the court, the justices' clerk must register the order in his court by entering it in the court register, specifying that the order is registered in accordance with s.6. Thereafter, it becomes as if it were an order of the court in which it is registered and may be enforced accordingly. The justices' clerk is empowered to take enforcement action in his own name, whether or not he is requested to do so by the person entitled to payment under the order. Indeed, by r.9(2) of the Magistrates' Courts (Reciprocal Enforcement) Rules 1974, there is an obligation placed upon the justices' clerk to bring enforcement action once four weeks' worth of arrears have accumulated (unless the justices' clerk feels that it would be unreasonable to do so).

It would seem that many cases have never had enforcement action taken, due to ignorance of this rule.

Where the order is expressed in a currency other than the United Kingdom currency, the equivalent exchange rate in sterling prevailing at the date of registration shall be the amount from thenceforth accruing due under the order. Any certificate of arrears which accompanies the order shall also be converted to sterling at the rate prevailing on the day of registration. Section 16(4) provides that a certificate signed by an officer of any United Kingdom Bank shall be evidence that a specified sum expressed in any overseas currency is equivalent to the sum expressed in sterling in the certificate.

Any order registered under this section may be varied under s.9 of the

Act of 1972; the procedure is dealt with later in this Guide under the heading "Variation and Revocation of Orders Registered in England and Wales". (See para.55 post).

51. **Jurisdiction of magistrates' courts in England and Wales to confirm provisional orders made in a reciprocating country — s.7 of the Act of 1972.**

The procedure under this section is virtually the same as the procedure outlined where overseas provisional orders are received by the justices' clerk under the provisions of s.4 of the Maintenance Orders (Facilities for Enforcement) Act 1920 (see para.31 ante), except for three important differences. These are:

(1) the order, if confirmed, either with or without alteration, is then required to be *registered* in the court of confirmation,

(2) the order is to be enforced in the same way as an affiliation order,

(3) the provisions of s.9 of the Act of 1972 (see para.55 hereof) apply as respects any applications to vary any order so confirmed and, accordingly, registered.

The order is to be registered by means of a memorandum entered and signed by the justices' clerk in the court register. In practice, however, justices' clerks would probably record the court's decision in words such as

"Order confirmed (with the following alteration, namely..........)
and registered in this court accordingly under s.7(5) of the Maintenance Orders (Reciprocal Enforcement) Act 1972."

or words to that effect.

52. **Non-service of summons**

Section 7(6) of the Act of 1972 provides that if it is not possible to serve a summons upon the respondent, the documents in the case are to be returned to the Home Office, with a statement giving such information as the justices' clerk has concerning the whereabouts of the respondent.

53. **Date of commencement of payments and application of law of reciprocating country.**

The court, in confirming a provisional order, shall specify the date from which the payments are to commence, being a date later than the making of the provisional order by the overseas court. In practice, no doubt, the date specified would either be the date of confirmation and registration or seven days (or one month) thereafter.

The order is to be treated as if it were originally made in the form in which it was confirmed, and as though it had never been a provisional order.

It should be noted that, in deciding whether or not to confirm the provisional order, the court is to decide the matter in accordance with the Law of the Reciprocating Country involved. The certificate from the overseas court will set out the grounds of defence open to the respondent under the reciprocating country's Law.

54. **Enforcement of orders registered in England and Wales — s.8 of the Act of 1972.**

All orders registered under Part 1 of the Act of 1972 are enforceable as though they were affiliation orders made by the court of registration, and justices' clerks are required to take the necessary steps for enforcement as if the order had been made in England or Wales. Unless the justices' clerk feels that it would be unreasonable so to do, he must bring enforcement action once four weeks' worth of arrears have accumulated, whether the person for whose benefit the payment should have been made requests him to do so or not. The justices' clerk is to proceed in his own name for the recovery of the arrears (see r. 9(2) of the Magistrates' Courts (Reciprocal Enforcement) Rules 1974.

55. **Variation and revocation or orders registered in England and Wales — s.9 of the Act of 1972.**

This section provides a complete machinery for varying and revoking orders registered in England and Wales — a feature which the 1920 Act failed to adequately provide for. It should be noted that the section applies to orders made in reciprocating countries under ss. 6 and 7 of the Act of 1972 (substantive orders made in reciprocating countries and provisional orders similarly made and which have been confirmed by and registered in magistrates' courts in England and Wales). However, the Registering court cannot vary a registered order, *except by means of a provisional order* unless:

1. Both the payer and the payee under the registered order are for the time being residing in the United Kingdom, or

2. The application is made by the *payee* under the registered order, or

3. The variation consists of a reduction in the rate of the payments under the order which is registered and is made solely on the ground that there has been a chance in the financial circumstances of the payer since the registered order was made, or, in the case of an order registered under s.7 of the Act of 1972, since the registered order was confirmed *and* the courts in the reciprocating country in which the maintenance order in question was made do not have power, according to the law in force in that country, to confirm provisional orders *varying* maintenance orders. (See column 4 of Appendix "B")

The registering court is not empowered to *revoke* a registered order, otherwise than by a provisional order, *unless both* the payer and the payee are for the time being residing in the United Kingdom. In deciding whether or not to make a provisional revocation order, that is, in cases where one or the other of the parties is still in a reciprocating country, the court is required to apply the law of the reciprocating country where the order was made. The court need not have before it expert evidence of the particular reciprocating country's law concerning the subject matter involved — it is merely sufficient that the court has reason to believe that the ground on which the application is made is a ground on which the order could be revoked according to the law in force in the reciprocating country. A letter of inquiry sent to the clerk of the court in the reciprocating country, setting out the grounds of the application, should elicit a reply to the effect that the particular ground is, or is not, a ground upon which the order may be revoked, if proved. The letter of reply, if in the affirmative, should be sufficient to give the magistrates' court in England and Wales "sufficient reason to believe" that the ground is a good ground upon which the order may be revoked.

Once the court has made a provisional variation order or a provisional revocation order, a certified copy thereof, together with the sworn depositions taken in evidence in support thereof, must be sent to the overseas court. In some cases, the documents may be sent direct to the court of origin overseas; in others, the documents must be forwarded via the Secretary of State. See Appendix "B" hereto.

If the provisional variation order is confirmed by the court in the reciprocating country, the justices' clerk, on receipt of a certified copy of the confirmation order, shall register it accordingly. If the provisional revocation order is confirmed by the overseas court, the justices' clerk, upon receipt of a certified copy of the confirmation order, shall cancel the original registration of the order. Only the arrears outstanding at the date of the cancellation of the registration may then be enforced.

56. **Power of magistrates' court to confirm provisional variation orders made in reciprocating countries.**

The magistrates' court is also empowered to entertain proceedings, by virtue of s.9(6) of the Act of 1972, for the confirmation of provisional variation orders which have been made by the court of origin in the reciprocating country. This provision enables, for example, a wife who resides in New Zealand to acquire an increase in her maintenance payment from her husband, where her husband is residing in England, and the original New Zealand order already stands registered in the English magistrates' court.

The provisional variation order, together with the evidence given in support thereof, may be received either direct from the overseas court, or may be transmitted to the registering court via the Home Office. The summons issued to the respondent to the application for the confirmation of the order shall recite the terms of the provisional order made overseas, and call upon the respondent to show cause why such order should not be confirmed, with or without such alteration as the magistrates' court thinks fit. It is suggested that a copy of the complainant's evidence be annexed to the summons so that the respondent will know the nature of the evidence already adduced in the proceedings overseas. The court has power to remit the case for the purpose of taking further evidence overseas, if necessary. The provisional variation order, if confirmed, with or without alteration, must be registered in the manner already described.

57. **Cancellation of registration — s. 10 of the Act of 1972.**

In cases where;

(1) a registered order is revoked by an order of the registering court,

(2) a registered order is revoked by a provisional order made by that court which has been confirmed by a court in a reciprocating country, and notice of confirmation is received by the registering court,

(3) a registered order is revoked by an order made by a court in a reciprocating country and notice of the revocation is received by the registering court,

the justices' clerk of the registering court must cancel the registration. However, any arrears due at the date of cancellation of registration may be recoverable.

The payer must be notified by the justices' clerk that registration has been cancelled.

The registration of an order registered under Part 1 of the Act of 1972 must also be cancelled if the justices' clerk in whose court the order is registered discovers that the payer is no longer residing within the jurisdiction of his court. Where the justices' clerk discovers that the payer is residing in another part of England or Wales he must send to the justices' clerk for that area:

1. A certified copy of the order, and a certificate of the arrears.
2. A statement giving such information as he possesses as to the whereabouts of the payer, and
3. Any relevant documents in his possession relating to the case.

The latter would, obviously, include certified copies of any variations to the original order.

The justices' clerk who receives the documents must take such steps as he thinks necessary in order to ascertain if the payer is, in fact, residing within his jurisdiction. If the payer is so residing, the justices' clerk shall register the order in his court in the manner hereinbefore described. (See para. 50 ante). He must also notify both the payer and the Secretary of State that the order has been registered in his court. Should the justices' clerk discover that the payer is not, after all, residing in his court area, he is required to send the order to the Secretary of State. Any information which the justices' clerk possesses about the whereabouts of the payer should also be sent to the Secretary of State.

Where, however, the justices' clerk in whose court the order is registered discovers that the payer is residing elsewhere than in England or Wales, he is required to send the order and the other documents referred to above to the Secretary of State so that the order may be registered in another reciprocating jurisdiction.

58. **Appeals — s. 12 of the Act of 1972.**

No appeal shall lie against the making of any provisional order by a magistrates' court in England or Wales under Part I of the Act of 1972. However, either party may appeal against justices' decisions to confirm, or refusal to confirm, orders under Part I of the Act. Similarly, where justices refuse to make a provisional order, the complainant may appeal; also, an appeal lies where justices vary an order or refuse to vary an order.

59. **Jurisdiction to proceed to vary without necessity of serving process — s. 17 of the Act of 1972.**

It should be noted that a summons, or other process is not necessary under Part I of the Act. Where the application is to vary and it is possible to make a provisional order of variation, that must be done. However, where the reciprocating court is in a country which does not have power to confirm provisional variation orders (see Appendix "B" hereto) the magistrates' court in England and Wales is empowered to vary the order absolutely under s.9(2)(c) of the Act of 1972 without the necessity of serving process under the provisions of the Magistrates' Courts Act 1980. (See para.55 ante).

60. Transitional provisions — s.23 & 24 of the Act of 1972.

Orders already registered under the 1920 Act in the High Court may be transferred by the HIgh Court to the magistrates' court for registration upon the country in which the order was made becoming a reciprocating country for the purposes of Part I of the 1972 Act. The justices' clerk shall register the order accordingly and cancel any registration in respect of the order under the Maintenance Orders Act 1958. Similarly, provision is made for orders already confirmed or registered under the 1920 Act to be re-registered under the appropriate provision of the 1972 Act upon the countries of origin becoming designated under the latter Act.

61. **THE MAINTENANCE ORDERS (RECIPROCAL ENFORCEMENT) ACT 1972 — PART II. CONVENTION COUNTRIES.**

This part of the Act is a result of the United Kingdom becoming a party to the United Nations Convention on the Recovery Abroad of Maintenance done at New York on the 20th June 1956. An entirely new concept with regard to the reciprocal recovery of maintenance with foreign countries is introduced. Unlike orders dealt with under Part 1 of the Act, proceedings for, and enforcement of, orders under Part 11 of the Act is in accordance with the law of the country where the respondent is residing. Therefore, a complainant residing in England or Wales will have to ensure that her application to recover maintenance from a husband or putative father residing in a "Convention Country" is made in accordance with the law in force in the relevant convention country. Conversely, applications by complainants residing in a convention country against persons residing in England and Wales will be determined in accordance with our own law. Thus, for example, an application by a married woman residing in a convention country for a maintenance order for herself and child against her husband residing in England and Wales will be treated for the purpose of the proceedings here as an application under Section 2 of the Domestic Proceedings and Magistrates' Courts Act 1978, and, similarly, an application for maintenance against a putative father will be treated as an application under the Affiliation Proceedings Act 1957.

A list of the convention countries to which the Act has been extended is contained in Appendix "C" hereto. The Act has been modified in its application to the United States of America. See, therefore, para.90 (post) and Appendix "D" where proceedings are contemplated in the United States courts.

62. **Application by a person in England or Wales for recovery of maintenance from a person residing in a convention country (s.26 of the Act of 1972)**

An appropriate form of complaint, and a form of questionnaire setting out the testimony in support of the complaint is annexed to Home Office Circular No.54/1975. (Forms 5,6 and 7 in the Forms Section of this Guide)

It should be noted that this section of the Act applies to all claims for maintenance, whether by a spouse for herself and children, or by the mother of an illegitimate child.

Where the applicant has an existing maintenance order or affiliation order made in the United Kingdom, the application is not made for recognition and enforcement of that order. It will merely be recognized in the Convention country that an obligation to support was established in the transmitting country. An application can only be treated as a claim for maintenance to be determined under the law of the Convention country where the respondent lives. An application for a variation of maintenance which is being paid by a person in a Convention country is treated as a claim in exactly the same way.

In regard to determination of paternity, it should be noted that, by s.44

of the Act of 1972, the court has no power to order blood tests under s.20 of the Family Law Reform Act 1969, but this exclusion does not operate so as to prevent any report carried out on blood tests to be received in evidence.

The application by the complainant for the recovery of maintenance, or for variation of an existing order, is to be made in the first instance through the justices' clerk, who has a statutory duty to assist the complainant in completing an application which will comply with the law applied in the appropriate convention country. The justices' clerk must then send the completed documents to the Secretary of State for transmission to the appropriate receiving agency in the convention country.

The fact that an order may already have been made in the United Kingdom does not materially alter the nature of the initial application. There is no provision for registering an existing United Kingdom order in the convention country, as is the case under Part I of the Act in its application to reciprocating countries, but the fact that an order is already in force can materially shorten the procedural matters to be adopted by the justices' clerk in the preparation of material to be transmitted to the Secretary of State.

In the vast majority of cases, the complainant will, no doubt, consult a solicitor, who will obtain the appropriate form of complaint and questionnaire from the justices' clerk. The completion of the form of complaint (or claim) and the accompanying questionnaire presents no difficulty. Where an order of a United Kingdom court is already in force, all that is necessary is to attach the order, duly authenticated, to the completed form of complaint and questionnaire. To the question "What, briefly, are the grounds for your claim?" in the case of an applicant who is a married woman, with, or without children, the answer can be, simply, "That the respondent has failed to comply with the order, and that the respondent has a legal duty under the law in force in the United Kingdom to maintain the applicant and/or her children" or as the case may be. A certificate of arrears should be attached. Similarly, in affiliation cases, it would be necessary to attach a duly authenticated copy of the affiliation order and certificate of arrears.

However, where there is no order of a United Kingdom court in force, the position is different. The applicant will have to adduce sworn testimony to prove her claim, and therefore, opposite the question set out above should appear the words "As set out in the affidavit(s) annexed hereto".

Applicants for the equivalent of an affiliation order in a convention country should be required to provide the justices' clerk with statements containing exactly the same evidence, including the necessary corroboration, as would be necessary to obtain an affiliation order in England and Wales. The birth certificate of the child, and documents material to the case, should be made exhibits. In the case of a married woman, she should be required to produce statements containing sufficient evidence to substantiate a claim on any one or more of the grounds contained in s.1 of the Domestic Proceedings and Magistrates' Courts Act 1978, or, where appropriate, the Guardianship of Minors Act 1971. Here again, the marriage certificate, birth certificates of any children, and any other documentary evidence should be made exhibits. Where the applicant has a solicitor, the solicitor should be requested to lodge them with the justices' clerk. Where the applicant has no solicitor, it would be the duty of the justices' clerk to assist the applicant in the preparation of the documents. In any event, whether the applicant is legally represented or not, there is a statutory duty cast upon the justices' clerk to assist the applicant. Once the justices' clerk has satisfied himself that the papers are in order, it is recommended that he arranges for the applicant and any witnesses to appear before the court, or indeed, before the justices' clerk himself, so that the complaint, questionnaire form and statements can be read to the complainant, and she will swear on oath as to the truth of the facts contained therein, and sign them accordingly in the presence of the justice or justices' clerk. The justice or justices' clerk will also add his signature. Any witnesses in support of the complainant's case should be called, and sworn, in the same manner. The hearing would, of course, be ex parte and in private.

Where the complainant, being the mother of the child or children for whom she is seeking maintenance, has married, or re-married, it is recommended that an affidavit by her husband setting out his means, where appropriate, should also be included with the documents. The reason for this is that the questionnaire merely asks for the complainant's income and expenditure, and if an affidavit by the present husband is not included, the documents transmitted to the convention court will not reflect the complainant's true financial position. Such a situation could result in the matter being sent back by the convention court for further evidence, thus resulting in considerable delay in finalising the matter.

When the above procedures have been completed, the documents should then be sent by the justices' clerk to the Secretary of State, who, if satisfied that the claim is made in good faith, and is in accordance with the law of the convention country concerned, will transmit them to the receiving agency overseas.

The foregoing procedure should be sufficient to establish that the claim is made in good faith, and would probably be acceptable in most, if not all, of the convention countries to which the Act applies.

It should be remembered that the application is made by the complainant to the Secretary of State. The justices' clerk and the court are merely the instruments by whom the material for the case is prepared and transmitted to the Secretary of State.

The complainant must make the application through the justices' clerk for the area where the complainant is residing.

A fact which cannot be emphasized often enough is that it is a misconception to suppose that an existing United Kingdom maintenance order will be recognized and enforced abroad in a Convention Country to which Part II of the 1972 Act applies (being the Countries set out in Appendix "C" hereto). It does sometimes happen that a foreign court (particularly in the U.S.A.) gives effect to the U.K. order by making its own order in identical terms, but this is not common. The essence of the procedure under Part II of the Act of 1972 is to establish afresh the liability to maintain (for which the U.K. court order provides important evidence) and to obtain a new maintenance order abroad.

63.   **Duty of court to take further evidence when required.**
    The Secretary of State is empowered to request the justices' clerk who transmits the application to obtain from his court such information about the application as may be specified in the request, and the court has a duty

to supply the information so required.

If the court in the convention country requires further evidence, the Secretary of State will request either the justices' clerk himself, or the court, to take the further evidence required. The power is contained in s.38 of the Act of 1972. Rules 9 and 10 of the Maigstrates' Courts (Recovery Abroad of Maintenance) Rules, 1975 prescribe the method by which the evidence is to be recorded. The method of taking the evidence and identifying any of the exhibits produced, is exactly the same as the taking of depositions in "old style" committals in indictable offences. Provision is made for the issue of witness summonses, and the payment of witnesses' expenses out of public funds, except that no payment of witness expenses shall be made to the complainant, if called to give further evidence.

64. **Function of justices' clerk.**

If an order is made in a convention country, it will be an order made in accordance with the law of that country, and the justices' clerk will have no authority to enforce it. His sole function in the matter would be to transmit any further claims by the complainant for variation of the order, or, at the direction of the Secretary of State, to take any further evidence which may be required by the overseas court.

65. **Application by person in a convention country for recovery of maintenance in England and Wales — s.27 of the Act of 1972**

This section deals with the situation where a claimant in a convention country desires to obtain maintenance from a person residing in England or Wales. The documents in the case will, in the first instance, have been transmitted to the Secretary of State who, in turn, will forward them to the justices' clerk for the area where the respondent is residing.

The application by the claimant in the convention country is to be treated as if it were a complaint, and a summons to the respondent is to be issued accordingly. Although, naturally, the documents transmitted from overseas will not name the English statute under which the proceedings are being instituted, it will be obvious to the receiving court the Statute under which the summons is to be issued. For example, a deserted wife will be claiming relief under s.2 of the Domestic Proceedings and Magistrates' Courts Act 1978 for herself and children. If claiming relief against her husband for the children only, the proceedings would be under the Guardianship of Minors Act 1971.

Similarly, the Affiliation Proceedings Act 1957 would be the appropriate statute where the claim is by the mother against the putative father of her child.

In cases where the application is for an affiliation order, s.27(2) gives the court for the commission area where the alleged putative father is residing jurisdiction to hear the complaint.

Unlike cases remitted from reciprocating countries abroad, under Part I of the Act, cases remitted from abroad under this section are determined in accordance with the law of England and Wales.

If a summons cannot be served upon the respondent, the documents must be returned to the Secretary of State. If the justices' clerk discovers that the respondent is residing in the United Kingdom, but outside England and Wales, he must inform the Secretary of State of this fact when returning the documents. If, however, the justices' clerk discovers that the respondent is residing in another petty sessions area in England or Wales, he must send the papers in the case to the justices' clerk for that area who then becomes seized of the matter. The justices' clerk to whom the papers were originally sent must notify the Secretary of State of the name and address of the justices' clerk to whom the papers have been forwarded.

At the hearing of the summons, the court is to proceed as if the complainant were before the court. In affiliation cases, where the time for the making of the complaint is crucial, it will be sufficient if it is proved to the court that the putative father had within three years after the birth of the child paid money for its maintenance in pursuance of the law applied by a court outside the United Kingdom.

It is recommended that a footnote be attached to the summons to the effect that a copy of the evidence transmitted from overseas will be supplied or made available to the defendant or his legal representative before the hearing. If, at the hearing, the defendant does not appear, the court, upon being satisfied that the summons has been duly served upon him, may proceed in his absence.

The proceedings should be commenced by the clerk reading out all the evidence adduced by the complainant, and then calling upon the defendant to answer to the complaint. The proceedings should follow as nearly as possible the procedure for the hearing of complaints in the ordinary way.

If the magistrates are able to come to a proper conclusion on the facts before them they can then either dismiss the complaint or make an order upon the complaint. If an order is made, the amounts to be paid thereunder must be expressed in sterling.

66. **Power of magistrates' court to require further evidence.**

If the magistrates are of opinion that they are unable to come to a conclusion on the facts before them, and wish to have further evidence from abroad, either from a particular witness (who may, or may not, already have given evidence by way of sworn affidavit) or perhaps, the complainant's answer to certain allegations made by the defendant, the court can request the Secretary of State to obtain from the appropriate court overseas further evidence about such matters as are specified in their request. The magistrates' court would then adjourn the case until such further evidence is available. The power to obtain such further evidence is contained in s.37 of the Act of 1972. Upon adjourning, the court would, if it considers it appropriate, have power to make an interim maintenance order.

67. **Representation of complainant in complex cases and lack of power of magistrates' court to refer to High Court.**

There is no power for the justices' to dismiss the case on the ground that it is more suitable for determination by the High Court.

In cases where the magistrates' court wishes to have the benefit of legal argument from both sides in a complex matter, it should ask the Secretary of State to arrange for the complainant to be legally represented, in accordance with the Power of Attorney given by the complainant under the United Nations Convention.

However, notwithstanding the guidance contained in para.9 of Home Office Circular 54/1975, magistrates' courts are not advised, unless they consider it *absolutely essential*, to ask the Secretary of State to arrange for the claimant to be legally aided. Experience has shown that the process of obtaining legal aid for a claimant overseas is complicated and time consuming and can create more problems than it solves.

68. **Registration of order.**

If an order is made on the complaint, it must be registered in the court in which it is made by means of a minute or memorandum entered in the court register and signed by the justices' clerk.

The memorandum must specify the Act, section and subsection under which the order is registered. Payments of sums due under an order so registered is to be made to the justices' clerk of the registering court, and the justices' clerk shall pay such sums to the person or authority nominated by the Secretary of State. (Magistrates' Courts (Recovery Abroad of Maintenance) Rules 1975).

69. **Taking of notes of evidence.**

In a contested case, it is vital that a full note of the evidence for the defence be taken, preferably by way of deposition, so that if the matter is referred back to the convention court, via the Secretary of State, for the taking of further evidence, a certified copy of the evidence already taken can accompany the request for further evidence; this information, along with the details specified in the request, will give the overseas authority some idea as to why the magistrates' court in England or Wales considers further evidence necessary.

70. **Convention order to be limited to maintenance and/or lump sum**

By s.28 of the Act of 1972, once the magistrates' court has decided to make an order upon the complaint, it is limited to making an order for maintenance only, including, if it thinks fit, payment of a lump sum.

71. **Custody and supervision orders.**

The magistrates' court has no jurisdiction to make orders regarding supervision of children, custody, access etc. In proceedings where the court has no jurisdiction to make a maintenance order, unless it also makes a custody order in respect of a child, the complainant is deemed to be the person to whom the legal custody of the child has been committed by an order of the court.

72. **Proceedings to be "Domestic Proceedings" within the meaning of the Magistrates' Courts Act 1980.**

Since the proceedings authorised by virtue of ss. 27 and 28 of the Act of 1972 will, invariably, be under either s.2 of the Domestic Proceedings and Magistrates' Courts Act 1978, the Guardianship of Minors Act 1971, or the Affiliation Proceedings Act 1957, such proceedings will be "Domestic Proceedings" within the meaning of s.65 of the Magistrates' Courts Act 1980. A full note of the evidence must, therefore, be taken in case of an appeal. In short, a magistrates' court must deal with the matter as though both parties were residing in England or Wales, and, therefore, subject to the exceptions noted above, must look for the same criteria to find the case proved as it would in the ordinary way in domestic cases. For example, the court must have regard to s.3 of the Domestic Proceedings and Magistrates' Courts Act 1978 when awarding maintenance for a wife and children; it must find that the necessary corroboration exists in affiliation cases, and so on.

73. **Requirement to give notice of making of order, or notice of dismissal of complaint and reasons for dismissal.**

Rule 4 of the Magistrates' Courts (Recovery Abroad of Maintenance) Rules 1975 requires that where a magistrates' court dismisses a complaint for maintenance under s.27 of the Act of 1972, or a complaint for a variation of an existing order, the justices' clerk shall send written notice to the Secretary of State of that fact, and shall also include in the notice a statement of the justices' reasons for their decision. Rule 6 of the above Rules requires the justices' clerk to send written notice to the Secretary of State of the fact that an order made in pursuance of a complaint transmitted under s.27 has been duly made and registered.

74. **Divorced spouse**

For the position where the claimant is a former spouse, see s.28A of the Act of 1972, which is dealt with in the next paragraph.

75. **Complaint by former spouse in convention country for recovery of maintenance in England and Wales from other spouse. Section 28A of the Act of 1972.**

This section has been added to the existing framework of the 1972 Act by s.58 of the Domestic Proceedings and Magistrates' Courts Act 1978.

Section 28A provides as follows:-

(1) Where on an application made under s.27(1) of the Act for recovery of maintenance from a person who is residing in England and Wales.

(a) that person is a former spouse of the applicant in a convention country who is seeking to recover maintenance, and

(b) the marriage between the applicant and the former spouse has been dissolved by a divorce granted in a convention country which is recognized as valid by the law of England and Wales, and

(c) an order for payment of maintenance for the benefit of the applicant or a child or the family has, by reason of the divorce proceedings in the convention country, been made by the court which granted the divorce or by any other court in that country,

the application shall, notwithstanding that the marriage has been dissolved, be treated as a complaint for an order under s.2 of the Domestic Proceedings and Magistrates' Courts Act 1978, and the provisions of this Section shall have effect.

(2) On hearing a complaint by virtue of this section, the magistrates' court may, if satisfied that the defendant has failed to comply with the provisions of any such order as is mentioned in sub-section (1)(c) above, make any Order which it has power to make under s.2 or s.19(1)(i) of the Domestic Proceedings and Magistrates' Courts Act 1978, except that

(a) an order for the making of periodical payments for the benefit of the applicant or any child of the family shall not be made unless the order made in the convention country provides for the making of periodical payments for the benefit of the applicant, or, as the case may be, that child, and

(b) an order for the payment of a lump sum for the benefit of the applicant or any child of the family shall not be made unless the order made in the convention country provides for the payment of a lump sum to the applicant, or, as the case may be, to that child.

(3) Part I of the Domestic Proceedings and Magistrates' Courts Act 1978 shall apply in relation to any application which is treated by virtue of this section as a complaint for an order under s.2 of that Act and in relation to any order made on the complaint, subject to the following modifications, that is to say:

(a) Section I shall be ommited. (Grounds of application for financial provision)

(b) for the reference in s.2(1) to any ground mentioned in s.1 of that Act, there shall be substituted a reference to non-compliance with any such order as is mentioned in subs. (1)(c) of this section.

(c) In s.3(1) for the reference to the occurrence of the conduct which is alleged as the ground of the application, there shall be substituted a reference to the breakdown of the marriage.

(d) In s.4(2) the reference to the subsequent dissolution or annulment of the marriage of the parties affected by the order shall be ommited.

(e) Ss. 6 to 18, 19(1)(ii), 21, 23(1), 24 to 28, 32(2) 33 and 34 shall be omitted.

(4) A divorce obtained in a convention country shall be presumed for the purposes of this section to be one the validity of which is recognized by the law of England and Wales, unless the contrary is proved by the defendant.

(5) The reference in subs. (1)(b) above to the dissolution of a marriage by divorce shall be construed as including a reference to the annulment of the marriage and any reference in this section to a divorce or to divorce proceedings shall be contrued accordingly.

(6) In this section the expression "child of the family" has the same meaning as in s.88 of the Domestic Proceedings and Magistrates' Courts Act 1978.

76. Transfer, Enforcement, Variation and Revocation of registered orders — s.32 of the Act of 1972.

(1) Where the prescribed officer of the registering court is of opinion that the payer under a registered order has ceased to reside within the jurisdiction of that court, then, unless he is of opinion that the payer has ceased to reside in the United Kingdom, he shall, subject to subs. (2) below, send a certified copy of the order and the related documents to the Secretary of State, and if he is of opinion that the payer has ceased to reside in the United Kingdom he shall send notice to that effect to the Secretary of State.

(2) Where the clerk of the registering court, being a magistrates' court, is of opinion that the payer is residing within the jurisdiction of another magistrates' court in that part of the United Kingdom in which the registering court is, he shall transfer the order to that other court by sending a certified copy of the order and the related documents to the clerk of that other court, and subject to subs. (4) below, that clerk shall register the order in the prescribed manner in that court.

(3) Where a certified copy of an order is received by the Secretary of State under this section and it appears to him that the payer under the order is still residing in the United Kingdom he shall transfer the order to the appropriate court by sending a copy of the order and the related documents to the prescribed officer of the appropriate court and, subject to subs. (4) below, that officer shall register the order in the prescribed manner in that court.

(4) Before registering an order in pursuance of subs. (2) or (3) above, an officer of the court shall take such steps as he thinks fit for the purpose of ascertaining whether the payer under the order is residing within the jurisdiction of the court, and if after taking those steps he is satisfied that the payer is not so residing he shall return the certified copy of the order and the related documents to the officer of the court or the Secretary of State, as the case may be, from whom he received them, together with a statement giving such information as he possesses as to the whereabouts of the payer.

(5) Where a certified copy of an order is received by the Secretary of State under this section and it appears to him that the payer under the order has ceased to reside in the United Kingdom, he shall return the copy of the order and the related documents to the registering court.

(6) An officer of a court on registering an order in the court in pursuance of subs. (2) or (3) above shall give notice of the registration in the prescribed manner to the prescribed officer of the court in which immediately before its registration under this section the order was registered.

(7) The officer to whom notice is given under subs. (6) above shall on receiving the notice cancel the registration of the order in that court.

(8) In this section —

"the appropriate court" in relation to a person residing in England and Wales or in Northern Ireland, means a magistrates' court within the jurisdiction of which that person is residing: "certificate of arrears" and "certified copy" have the same meanings respectively as in Part I of this Act;

"payer" in relation to a registered order means the person liable to make payments under the order, and "related documents" means —

(a) the application on which the order was made;

(b) a certificate of arrears signed by the prescribed officer of the registering court;

(c) a statement giving such information as he possesses as to the whereabouts of the payer; and

(d) any relevant documents in his possession relating to the case.

Rule 5 of the Magistrates' Courts (Recovery Abroad of Maintenance) Rules 1975 provides as follows:-

(1) Where a magistrates' court makes an order which is required under s.27(8) of the Act to be registered, the justices' clerk shall enter and sign a minute or memorandum of the order in his register.

(2) Where a justices' clerk in pursuance of s.32(2) or (3) of the Act (transfer of orders) receives a certified copy of an order he shall cause the order to be registered in his court by means of a minute or memorandum entered and signed by him in his register.

(3) Every minute or memorandum entered in pursuance of para. (1) or

(2) above shall specify the section and subsection of the Act under which the order in question is registered.

It should be noted that by reason of subs. (4) and (5) above where the order is returned to the justices' clerk of the registering court, following an attempt to cause the order to be registered elsewhere, the order then remains registered in the court of the justices' clerk who sought to cause the re-registration of the order, notwithstanding that the payer may have left the United Kingdom.

Rule 6 of the Magistrates' Courts (Recovery Abroad of Maintenance) Rules 1975 provides as follows:-

(1) Where a justices' clerk registers an order in pursuance of s.27(8) or s.32(2) or (3) of the Act, he shall send written notice to the Secretary of State that the order has been duly registered.

(2) Where a justices' clerk is required by s.32(6) of the Act to give notice of the registration of an order he shall do so by sending written notice to the officer specified in that subsection that the order has been duly registered.

77. **Enforcement of Orders Registered under Part II of the Act of 1972.**

Section 33 of the Maintenance Orders (Reciprocal Enforcement) Act 1972 provides as follows:-

(1) Subject to subs. (2) below, a registered order which is registered in a court other than the court by which the order was made may be enforced as if it had been made by the registering court and as if that court had had jurisdiction to make it; and proceedings for or with respect to the enforcement of any such order may be taken in accordance with this subsection but not otherwise.

(2) Subsection (1) above does not apply to an order which is for the time being registered in the High Court under Part I of the Maintenance Orders Act 1958, or to an order which is for the time being registered in the High Court of Justice in Northern Ireland under Part II of the Maintenance and Affiliation Orders Act (Northern Ireland) 1966.

(3) An order which by virtue of subsection (1) above is enforceable by a Magistrates' Court shall be enforceable as if it were an affiliation order made by that court; and the provisions of any enactment with respect to the enforcement of affiliation orders (including enactments relating to the accrual of arrears and the remission of sums due) shall apply accordingly.

In this subsection "enactment" includes any order, rule, or regulation made in pursuance of any Act.

(4) A magistrates' court in which an order is registered under this Part of this Act, and the officers thereof, shall take all such steps for enforcing the order as may be prescribed.

(Note: see r.7 quoted below)

(5) In any proceedings for or with respect to the enforcement of an order which is for the time being registered in any court under this part of this Act a certificate of arrears sent under s.32 of this Act to the prescribed officer of the Court shall be evidence of the facts stated therein.

(6) Part II of the Maintenance Orders Act 1950 (enforcement of certain orders throughout the United Kingdom) shall not apply to a registered order.

78   Rule 7 of the Magistrates' Courts (Recovery Abroad of Maintenance) Rules 1975 deals with the enforcement of orders registered under Part II. The said Rule 7 provides as follows:-

(1) Payments of sums due under registered orders shall, while the order is registered in a magistrates' court, be made to the clerk of the registering court during such hours and at such place as that clerk may direct; and a justices' clerk to whom payments are made under this rule shall send those payments by post to such person or authority as the Secretary of State may from time to time direct.

(2) Where it appears to a justices' clerk to whom payments under a registered order are made by virtue of paragraph (1) above that any sums under the order are in arrears, he may, and, if such sums are in arrear to an amount equal:

(a) in the case of payments to be made monthly or less frequently, to twice the sum payable periodically, or

(b) in any other case, to four times the sum payable periodically, he shall, whether the person for whose benefit the payment should have been made requests him to do so or not, proceed in his own name for the receovery of those sums, unless it appears to him that it is unreasonable in the circumstances to do so.

It will be noted from the above rule that there is *an obligation* placed upon the justices' clerk to enforce the order *without first obtaining the payee's authorization.*

Although the orders must be made in sterling, the view of the Home Office working party on Magistrates' Courts is that payments should be sent abroad in the currency of the Convention country. The cost of exchanging sterling to that currency ranks for grant.

79   **Exclusion of all other methods of enforcement of convention orders registered under Part II of the Act of 1972 apart from that authorised by s.33 of the Act.**

The effect of s.33 is that every order registered under Part II of the Act of 1972 is enforceable in a magistrates' court as if it were an affiliation order, and the order is only enforceable in accordance with the provisions of the said s.33. (See paras. 77 and 78 ante.)

80.   **Appropriate court to enforce convention order.**

If the order is registered in a court other than the court which made it, the registering court shall have full power to enforce the order. Where the order is re-registered in the High Court under the Maintenance Orders Act 1958 (or in the Northern Irish High Court) it is the High Court which will enforce the order — the magistrates' court does not retain power to enforce it.

81.   **Non-application of Maintenance Orders Act 1950 to convention orders.**

If the order is registered in a magistates' court in England or Wales, and the payer moves to Scotland or Northern Ireland, the order cannot be registered in those countries by reason of Part II of the Maintenance Orders Act 1950 because adequate provision for the transfer of orders is provided for by s.32 of the Act of 1972. Part II of the Act of 1950 is, therefore, dis-applied to "Convention Orders". (see para. 76 ante.)

82. **Variation and revocation of Convention orders — s.34 of the Act of 1972.**
     Section 34 of the Act of 1972 provides as follows:-
     (1) Where a registered order is registered in a court other than the court by which the order was made, the registering court shall have the like power to vary or revoke the order as if it had been made by the registering court and as if that court had had jurisdiction to make it; and no court other than the registering court shall have power to vary or revoke a registered order.
     (2) Where the registering court revokes a registered order it shall cancel the registration.
     (3) Where the Secretary of State receives from the appropriate authority in a convention country an application by a person in that country for the variation of a registered order, he shall, if the registering court is a magistrates' court, send the application together with any documents accompanying it to the clerk of that court.
     (4) Where a court in a part of the United Kingdom makes, or refuses to make, an order varying or revoking a registered order made by a court in another part thereof, any person shall have the like right of appeal (if any) against the order or refusal as he would have if the registered order had been made by the first-mentioned court.

83. **Retention of power to vary affiliation order on application of third party.**
     In regard to affiliation orders, s.30(5) of the Act of 1972 preserves the situation, in its application to "Convention Orders", that affiliation orders may be varied on an application by a third person having the custody of the illegitimate child so that the payments may be made to the person having the custody of the child.

84. **Further provisions with respect to variation etc., of orders by magistrates' courts — s.35 of the Act of 1972.**
     Section 35 of the Act provides as follows:-
     (1) Notwithstanding anything in s.28, 28A (3) (e) or s.30(6) of this Act, a magistrates' court shall have jurisdiction to hear an application for the variation or revocation of a registered order registered in that court, being —
           (a) an application made by the person against whom or on whose application the order was made, or
           (b) an application made by some other person in pursuance of s.30(5) of this Act for the variation of an affiliation order,
     notwithstanding that the person by or against whom the application is made is residing outside England and Wales.
     (2) Where an application by a person in a convention country for the variation of a registered order is received from the Secretary of State by the clerk of a magistrates' court, he shall treat the application as if it were a complaint for the variation of the order to which the application relates, and the court hearing the application shall proceed as if the application were a complaint and the applicant were before the court.
     (3) Without prejudice to subs. (2) above, an application to a magistrates' court for the variation or revocation of a registered order shall be made by complaint.
     (4) Where the defendant to a complaint for the variation or revocation

of a registered order, being an order registered in a magistrates' court, does not appear at the time and place appointed for the hearing of the complaint, but the court is satisfied —

(a) that the defendant is residing outside England and Wales; and

(b) that such notice of the making of the complaint and of the time and place aforesaid as may be prescribed has been given to the defendant in the prescribed manner,

the court may proceed to hear and determine the complaint at the time and place appointed for the hearing or for any adjourned hearing in like manner as if the defendant had appeared at that time and place.

(5) This section shall have effect in Northern Ireland with the substitution of references to Northern Ireland for references to England and Wales.

85. Meaning of "registered order" under Part II of the Act of 1972.

The "Registered Orders" referred to in Part II of the Act of 1972 relate only to orders which are in fact registered under the said Part II, being convention orders. They should not be confused with orders registered under Part I (Reciprocal Orders) or, indeed, with the orders registered under the Maintenance Orders (Facilities for Enforcement) Act 1920.

86. Code of procedure for variation etc., of registered orders (Convention countries).

Section 35 sets out its own code of procedure for variation and revocation of registered orders. This section dis-applies all other modes of procedure for variation of all orders to which Part II of the Act applies.

87. Practical effect of s.26(2) and s.35 of the Act.

The practical effect of s.26(2) and s.35 in relation to revocation and variation of "Convention Maintenance Orders" is:

1. Where a complainant residing in England or Wales who has obtained an order in a convention country, desires to obtain an increase in that order, the application will have to be lodged under s.26(2) of the Act, and the same procedure will have to be followed as that which applies to an application for an original order in the convention country.

2. Where the complainant is residing in a convention country, the justices' clerk will receive the application to vary via the Secretary of State with the accompanying evidence. The justices' clerk will treat the application as a complaint and issue a summons to the respondent, and the matter will be determined in the ordinary way. Only the magistrates' court in which the order is registered for the time being will have the power to vary it. A request for further evidence, if necessary, may be made under s.37 of the Act, in the same way as an application for an original order.

(3) Where, for example, a husband or putative father is residing in England or Wales, and a "Convention Order" has been made by a court in the United Kingdom, and that order has been registered in an English or Welsh Court, he may apply to the magistrates' court in which the order is registered for the order to be varied. Notice of the making of the application must be served upon the person entitled to payments in the prescribed manner. The service of such notice is prescribed by r.8 of the Magistrates' Courts (Recovery Abroad of Maintenance) Rules 1975

which provides as follows:

> 8(1) Notice under s.35(4) of the Act (variation of orders by magistrates' courts) of the making of a complaint for the variation or revocation of a registered order and of the time and place appointed for the hearing of the complaint shall be in the form specified in the schedule to these rules, (See form 10A) and shall be sent by post by the justices' clerk to the Secretary of State for onward transmission to the appropriate authority in the convention country in which the defendant is residing.
>
> (2) The time appointed for the hearing of the said complaint shall not be less than six weeks later than the date on which the said notice is sent to the Secretary of State.

Although the date fixed for the hearing must not be earlier than six weeks after the notice is sent to the Secretary of State, in practice it is sensible to arrange a hearing a good deal later than six weeks after the notice has been sent to the Secretary of State to allow time for Home Office officials to transmit the notice via the relevant central authority abroad and receive any response. Three months might be more appropriate.

88. Non-appearance of defendant.

If the defendant, having been given notice, does not appear, the court can proceed in his or her absence. However, if the defendant files with the court sworn evidence taken in the convention country, the court is entitled to take judicial notice of the sworn evidence as though the defendant were present, and had given oral evidence of the facts contained in the deposition.

89. Both parties accorded opportunity of being heard.

The advantage of the variation and revocation provisions under Part II of the Act is that there is no question of the court determining a matter without both parties being given an opportunity of being heard, either by way of personal appearance, or by way of sworn deposition.

90. The United States of America.

In the United States there exists a statute known as "The Uniform Reciprocal Enforcement of Support Act (1968)". It has been adopted by most, but not all, States. Section 14 of that Act provides, amongst other matters, as follows:-

"If the initiating court finds that the petition sets forth facts from which it may be determined that the obligor owes a duty of support and that a court of the Responding State may obtain jurisdiction of the obligor or his property, it shall so certify and cause three copies of the petition and its certificate and one copy of this Act to be sent to the Responding Court. Certification shall be in accordance with the requirements of the initiating State............"

In order to give effect to this requirement, Part II of the Act of 1972 of the United Kingdom Parliament has been modified insofar as it applies to the United States of America. Part II does not apply to all American States — those States to which the Act does apply are noted in Appendix "D" hereto.

The modification is effected by "The Recovery of Maintenance

(United States of America) Order 1979".

After s.26(3) of the Act of 1972, the 1979 Order adds a further subs., as follows:-

(3A) An application under subs. (1) or (2) above, for the purpose of recovering maintenance from a person in a specified State within the meaning of the Recovery of Maintenance (United States of America) Order 1979, and a certificate signed by a justice of the peace, or where the applicant is residing in Scotland, the sheriff, to the effect that the application sets forth facts from which it may be determined that the respondent owes a duty to maintain the applicant and any other person named in the application and that a court in the specified State may obtain jurisdiction of the respondent or his property shall be registered in the court in the prescribed manner by the appropriate officer, or in Scotland, by the sheriff clerk in the Maintenance Orders (Reciprocal Enforcement) Act 1972 register.

The Magistrates' Courts (Recovery Abroad of Maintenance) (Amendment) Rules 1979 provide that the Rules of 1975 shall apply to the specified States of the United States of America as they apply to every other convention country, but with the addition of a rule (rule 5A) which provides that where a claim for maintenance is made against a person residing in a convention state in the United States of America, the justices' clerk shall enter and sign a minute or memorandum of the application and certificate in his court register.

The Home Office, in Circular No. HOC 172/1979 of 31st December 1979, states that it will provide the necessary photo-copies of the application and Part II of the Act of 1972 to accompany the original documents when they are transmitted by the Home Office to the United States. The above circular also has annexed to it the appropriate form of "Petition for Support", "Testimony" "Certificate" and "Pauper's Affidavit". (See forms 8, 9 and 10 to this Guide). Since the application will have to be made in accordance with the appropriate American State Law, the Home Office recommends that these forms be used by the courts in this country in the preparation of the case.

All the documents must be sworn before a Justice of the Peace. The procedure suggested in para. 62 (ante) in regard to applications under the (unmodified) s.26 of the Act would therefore be particularly appropriate, except that applications must be sworn before a justice of the peace, and *not* before the justices' clerk.

It should be noted that the modification of Part II only affects applications made, insofar as England and Wales is concerned, by persons residing in England and Wales who wish to make a claim against persons residing in the United States of America.

Incoming applications from the United States of America are dealt with by the courts in England and Wales in accordance with the procedure as described in the main part of this Guide which deals with the operation of Part II of the Act, that is ss.27 to 35. (See paras. 65 to 89.)

91. **THE REPUBLIC OF IRELAND**

The Irish Republic has been designated a "Reciprocating Country" for the purposes of the Maintenance Orders (Reciprocal Enforcement) Act 1972, and, therefore, Part I of that Act applies to it.

However, Part I of the Act has been modified by the Reciprocal

Enforcement of Maintenance Orders (Republic of Ireland) Order 1974. (S.I. 1974 No.2140).

The full text of the modified Part I is set out in sch.2 of the Order.

For the purposes of the application of the Act to the Irish Republic, the references to Part I of the Act means Part I as so modified by the above mentioned Order of 1974. The Order came into force on April 1 1975.

A fundamental difference between the unmodified Part I and the modification of Part I referred to above is that it is the same magistrates' court which not only makes the provisional maintenance order, but also decides whether or not to confirm it, either with or without modification. The reciprocal arrangments with the Republic apply to all types of maintenance orders including affiliation orders.

92. **Transmission of maintenance order made in the United Kingdom for enforcement in the Republic of Ireland — s.2 of the Act as modified.**

(1) Subject to subs. (2) below, where the payer under a maintenance order made, whether before, on or after 1st April 1975 by a court in the United Kingdom is residing in the Republic of Ireland, the payee under the order may apply for the order to be sent to that country for enforcement.

(2) Subsection (1) above shall not have effect in relation to a provisional order or to an order made by virtue of a provision of Part II of this Act.

(3) Every application under this section shall be made in the prescribed manner to the prescribed officer of the court which made the maintenance order to which the application relates.

(4) If, on an application duly made under this section to the prescribed officer of a court in the United Kingdom, that officer is satisfied that the payer under the maintenance order to which the application relates is residing in the Republic of Ireland, the following documents, that is to say:-

(a) a certified copy of the maintenance order,

(b) a certificate signed by that officer certifying that the order is enforceable in the United Kingdom,

(c) a certificate of arrears so signed,

(d) a statement giving such information as the officer possesses as to the whereabouts of the payer,

(e) a statement giving such information as the officer possesses for facilitating the identification of the payer,

(f) where available, a photograph of the payer,

(g) if the payer did not appear in the proceedings in which the maintenance order was made, the original, or a certified copy of a document which establishes that notice of the institution of the proceedings was served on the payer,

(h) a document which establishes that notice of the order was sent to the payer, and

(i) if the payee received legal aid in the proceedings, a written statement to that effect signed by that officer,

shall be sent by that officer to the Secretary of State with a view to their being transmitted by the Secretary of State to the responsible authority in the Republic of Ireland if he is satisfied that the statement relating to the whereabouts of the payer gives sufficient information to justify that being done.

(5) Nothing in this section shall be taken as affecting any jurisdiction of a court in the United Kingdom with respect to a maintenance order to which this section applies, and any such order may be enforced, varied or revoked accordingly.

Rule 4 of the Magistrates' Courts (Reciprocal Enforcement of Maintenance Orders) (Republic Ireland) Rules 1975, provides that

(1) an application under s.2 of the Act (transmission of maintenance order made in the United Kingdom for enforcement in the Republic of Ireland) may, where the court which made the maintenance order to which the application relates is a magistrates' court, be made in writing by or on behalf of the payee under the order.

(2) any application made in pursuance of para.(1) above shall:

    (a) specify the date on which the order was made,

    (b) contain such particulars as are known to the applicant of the whereabouts of the payer,

    (c) specify any matters likely to assist in the identification of the payer,

    (d) where possible, be accompanied by a recent photograph of the payer,

(3) In this rule, "the payer" means the payer under the order to which the application relates.

93. Justices' clerk to be the prescribed officer of the Magistrates' Court.

By r.3 of the above cited Rules, the officer of any court, by or in relation to whom anything is to be done in pursuance of any provision of Part I of the Act shall, where that court is a magistrates' court, be the justices' clerk.

94. Transmission of county court order.

If the court which made the order is not a magistrates' court, application for transmission of the order to the Irish Republic must be made, not to the justices' clerk, but to the prescribed officer of the court which made the order, e.g., the registrar of the county court.

95. Power of magistrates' court to make and confirm provisional maintenance order against a person residing in the Republic of Ireland — s.3 of the Act as modified.

(1) Where a complaint is made to a magistrates' court against a person residing in the Republic of Ireland and the complaint is one on which the court would have jurisdiction by virtue of any enactment to make a maintenance order if —

    (a) that person were residing in England and Wales; and

    (b) a summons to appear before the court to answer to the complaint had been duly served on him,

the court shall have jurisdiction to hear the complaint and may, subject to subs.(2) below, make a maintenance order on the complaint.

(2) A maintenance order made by virtue of this section shall be a provisional order.

(3) If the court hearing a complaint to which subs. (1) above applies is satisfied —

    (a) that there are grounds on which a maintenance order

containing a provision requiring the making of payments for the maintenance of a child may be made on that complaint, but

(b) that it has no jurisdiction to make that order unless it also makes an order providing for the legal custody of that child,

then, for the purpose of enabling the court to make the maintenance order, the complainant shall be deemed to be the person to whom the legal custody of that child had been committed by an order of the court which is for the time being in force.

(4) No enactment empowering a magistrates' court to refuse to make an order on a complaint on the ground that the matter in question is one which would be more conveniently dealt with by the High Court shall apply in relation to a complaint to which subs.(1) above applies.

(5) Where a court makes a maintenance order which is by virtue of this section a provisional order, the following documents, that is to say:-

(a) A certified copy of the maintenance order; (form 3)

(b) a document authenticated in the prescribed manner setting out or summarising the evidence given in the proceedings;

(c) a certificate signed by the prescribed officer of the court certifying that the grounds stated in the certificate are the grounds on which the making of the order might have been opposed by the payer under the order; (Form 4)

(ca) a notice addressed to the payer stating that a provisional order has been made, that it has no effect unless and until confirmed with or without alteration by the court making the order, and that in considering whether or not to confirm the provisional order the court will take into account any representations made, or any evidence adduced by or on behalf of the pyaer within three weeks from the date of service of the notice; (Form 11)

(d) a statement giving such information as was available to the court as to the whereabouts of the payer;

(e) a statement giving such information as the officer possesses for facilitating the identification of the payer; and

(f) where available, a photograph of the payer;

shall be sent by that officer to the Secretary of State with a view to their being transmitted by the Secretary of State to the responsible authority in the Republic of Ireland if he is satisfied that the statement relating to the whereabouts of the payer gives sufficient information to justify that being done.

(6) The court which made a provisional order by virtue of this section shall not earlier than three weeks after the date of service of the notice referred to in para. (ca) of subs.(5) above consider whether or not to confirm the order and with or without alteration and shall take into account any representations made and any evidence adduced by or on behalf of the payer.

(6A) Where the payer makes any representations or adduces any evidence, a copy of the representations or evidence shall be served on the person on whose application the provisional order was made before the date of the hearing at which confirmation of the provisional order will be considered and that person shall be notified in the prescribed manner of the date fixed for the hearing.

(6B) The court shall not confirm such an order unless the documents mentioned in paras. (a) (b) (c) and (ca) of subs.(5) above have been served on the payer in accordance with the law for the service of such documents in the Republic of Ireland and in sufficient time to enable him to arrange for his defence.

(6C) Where an order has been confirmed under this section, the prescribed officer of the court shall —

    (a) send to the payer by registered post notice of the confirmation of the order; and

    (b) send the following documents, that is to say:-

        (i) a certified copy of the maintenance order as confirmed;

        (ii) a certificate signed by that officer certifying that the order is enforceable in the United Kingdom;

        (iii) if the payer did not appear in the proceedings in which the order was confirmed, the original or a certified copy of a document which establishes that the documents mentioned in paras. (a) (b) (c) and (ca) of subs.(5) above have been served on the payer;

        (iv) a document which establishes that notice of the confirmation of the order has been sent to payer by registered post;

        (v) if the payee received legal aid in the proceedings, a written statement to that effect signed by that officer;

to the Secretary of State with a view to their being transmitted by the Secretary of State to the responsible authority in the Republic of Ireland.

(6D) Where the court decides not to confirm a provisional order, it shall revoke the order.

(7) In the application of this section to Northern Ireland, in subs.(1), for the reference to England and Wales there shall be substituted a reference to Northern Ireland and in subs.(4) for the reference to the High Court there shall be substituted a reference to the High Court of Justice in Northern Ireland.

Notes:
The "prescribed officer" in relation to magistrates' courts is the justices' clerk.

Rule 5 of the Magistrates' Courts (Reciprocal Enforcement of Maintenance Orders) (Republic of Ireland) Rules 1975 provides that a document setting out or summarising any evidence required by s.3(5)(b) and s.5(2) of the Act to be authenticated shall be authenticated by a certificate signed by one of the justices before whom that evidence was given, that the document is the original document setting out or, as the case may be, summarising that evidence, or a true copy of that document. Rule 6 of the above cited Rules provides that where under s.3(6A) of the Act a person is required to be notified of the date fixed for the hearing at which confirmation of a provisional order is to be considred, the clerk to the magistrates' court which made the provisional order shall send that person written notice of the date fixed.

It should be particularly noted that the proceedings before the magistrates' court with a view to confirmation of its provisional order cannot take place earlier than three weeks following the service of the documents on the defendant in the Irish Republic, and the magistrates' court must not confirm the order unless it is satisfied that the required documents have been served on the defendant in the Republic in sufficient time to enable him to arrange for his defence. The clerk to the justices is required to serve on the complainant a copy of any representations or evidence adduced by the defendant in the Republic. These documents can be served at the same time as the notice to the complainant of the date of the hearing at which confirmation will be considered. It would also be necessary, of course, for the justices' clerk to notify the defendant, by post, of the date fixed for the "confirmation" hearing, although the Act and Rules do not specifically require this to be done.

The justices' clerk will receive from the authorities in the Republic a document or documents which will establish that service has been effected on the defendant, and the date of such service.

If the order is confirmed, the procedure set out in s.3(6C) must be followed strictly. If the order is not confirmed, the court must revoke the order.

96. **Procedure at the "Confirmation" hearing.**

What is the procedure to be followed at the "confirmation" hearing? There is nothing in the Act or the rules regulating the procedure. It is submitted that the same justices who made the provisional order should finally decide whether or not to confirm it. The original depositions can be read to the justices to remind them of the facts. If the defendant appears, either in person, or by way of legal representation, the complainant and her witnesses, if any, can then re-enter the witness box to be cross-examined. The defendant (if personally present) can then be called to give his evidence, and be cross-examined, and the same would apply to his witnesses, if any.

If the defendant chooses to put his defence before the court by way of evidence taken and sworn in the Republic, without making a personal appearance, his evidence, and that of any of his witnesses, must be read to the court.

It is submitted that the complainant should then be given the opportunity of replying to that evidence, and if any further evidence is required from the defendant, as a result of her reply to that evidence, the case should be further adjourned so that a request may be made for the taking of further evidence in the Republic from the defendant on specific points raised. Of course, all this takes time and can result in much delay before a final determination on whether or not to confirm the order is reached. The power to make such a request is conferred by s.14 of the Act of 1972 (as modified by the Reciprocal Enforcement of Maintenance Orders) (Republic of Ireland) Order 1974. See sch.2 to that order.

Where the defendant does not appear in person at the "confirmation" hearing, but nevertheless contests the confirmation of the provisional order by way of sworn affidavit, it is important, therefore, that any additional evidence is taken by way of deposition, duly signed and authenticated, so that it will be available for transmission to the authorities in the Republic, should a request for further evidence from the defendant be necessary. A copy of any such further evidence taken in the Republic should be served on the complainant in the same manner as that leading up to the first "confirmation" hearing.

97. **Variation and revocation of maintenance orders made in the United Kingdom — s.5 of the Act as modified.**

This section applies to all United Kingdom maintenance orders which have been registered in the Republic.

The procedure envisaged is quite simple. The complainant will file her complaint with the justices' clerk. An ex parte hearing is arranged at which the evidence in support will be taken by way of sworn deposition. The depositions will be authenticated by one of the justices before whom it was taken. A certified copy of the complaint, and the depositions, will then be sent to the Secretary of State for transmission to the Authorities in the Republic, with a view to service of the same upon the defendant. The magistrates' court must not determine the application until at least three weeks after the date when the application and depositions have been served on the defendant. If any representations or sworn evidence is received from the defendant, the court must take the same into account. The notes in para. 96 ante regarding the procedure to be followed would apply equally to the final "variation" hearing, as they would to a "confirmation" hearing under s.3.

Where such an order has been varied or revoked in accordance with this procedure a certified copy of the order of variation or revocation must be sent to the court in the Irish Republic by which it is being enforced, as well as a document containing a statement of the service of the process which lead to the variation or revocation. The Rules (r.7) prescribe that these documents shall be sent by post direct to the court in the Republic.

The variation or revocation is to be effective as from the date of such variation or revocation. The revocation of the order is not to have effect so as to preclude the enforcement of any arrears due at the date of revocation.

A copy of a variation or revocation order must be sent to the Secretary of State by the justices' clerk. (r.12).

98. **Registration in the United Kingdom of orders made in the Irish Republic. S.6 of the Act as modified.**

Maintenance orders made in the Irish Republic can be registered in magistrates' courts in England and Wales. Such orders will be received by the justices' clerk from the Secretary of State. The justices' clerk, upon receipt of the order from the Secretary of State, shall register the order in his court by means of a minute or memorandum entered and signed by him in the appropriate court register. Before registering the order, however, the justices' clerk must take such steps as he sees fit to ascertain whether the payer under the order is, in fact, residing within the jurisdiction of his court. The type and method of such inquiry is left to the discretion of the justices' clerk.

If it transpires that the payer is not residing in the area covered by the justices' clerk, the justices' clerk must return the papers to the Home Office and inform the Home Office of any other address at which the payer is residing, if he possesses such information.

Even if the payer is found to be in the area of the justices' clerk to whom the papers are sent, the justices' clerk *shall not register the order* if any one of the following circumstances are found to exist, namely:-

(1) If the registration of the order is contrary to public policy,

(2) If the payer did not appear in the proceedings in the Republic of

Ireland and he was not served in accordance with the law of the place where he was residing with the summons or other notice of the institution of the proceedings in sufficient time to enable him to arrange for his defence.

(3) If the order is irreconcilable with a judgment given in the United Kingdom in proceedings between the same parties.

In regard to para. (1) above, it was held in the case of *Armitage* v *Nanchen* (1983) 147 JP 53 that where a foreign decree is made in accordance with the proper procedures of the foreign law, and there is no fraud or similar delinquency involved in the case, the court will only reject the decree if the foreign law concerned is so offensive to the English conception that it would constitute an infraction of the rules of natural justice in the eye of the English Court for the decree to be the subject of recognition here. Insofar as para.(2) is concerned, the accompanying documents will establish whether or not this ground exists. Paragraph (3) will, in the first instance, present some difficulty to a justices' clerk unless he has some previous knowledge of the case. The justices' clerk is not required to institute an inquiry into the matters at (1) (2) or (3) above, but the section imposes a duty upon him to refuse registration if it appears to him that one or all of the above prohibitions exist.

99. **Right of appeal by payer against registration order.**

Having registered the order, the justices' clerk must then serve notice on the payer of the registration of the order. (See form 14). The payee must also be notified. The notice to the payer must be in the prescribed form, and the payer may appeal against the registration to the court of registration within one calendar month from the date of service of the notice. The appeal must be on one or more of the grounds mentioned in paras. (1) (2) and (3) above.

If the payer appeals to set aside the registration of the order, the justices' clerk must give notice to the payee of the appeal and the date when such appeal is to be heard.

Upon appealing, the payer may also apply to the court of registration to stay the proceedings if:

> (a) enforcement of the maintenance order has been suspended in the Republic of Ireland pending the determination of any form of appeal; or
>
> (b) the time for an appeal has not yet expired and enforcement has been suspended pending the making of an appeal,

but in the event of para.(b) above applying, the court of registration may lay down the time limit within which the proceedings will be stayed.

100. **Right of payee to appeal against refusal to register order.**

Just as the *payer* has a right of appeal against the justices' clerk's decision to *register* the order, the *payee* has an equal right to appeal against the justices' clerk's decision *not to register* the order. (See form 16). The justices' clerk must serve notice of his refusal to register on the payee (form 15). The appeal by the payee would be by way of complaint, and she and/or her legal representative would have to appear at the court hearing her appeal, since the appeal would be dealt with under the Magistrates' Courts Act 1980 and the rules thereunder; therefore, evidence by way of deposition or affidavit under s.14 of the Act of 1972 would be inapplicable.

An interesting point arises here inasmuch as that the appeal would be against the decision of the justices' clerk. How far should he, or a member of his staff, advise the justices on the issue? Should a neighbouring justices' clerk be called in to sit as clerk? The answer is probably "Yes" for justice to be seen to be done.

101. **Suspension of enforcement pending appeal against registration.**

While an appeal against registration is pending, or during the time within which an appeal against registration may be lodged, no action to enforce the order may be taken other than such action as is designed to protect the interests of the payee, but this provision will not prevent such an order being registered in the High Court under Part I of the Maintenance Orders Act 1958.

102. **Enforcement of maintenance order registered in United Kingdom s.8 of the Act as modified.**

It may happen that only part of a Republic order is enforceable in the United Kingdom. In that event the magistrates' court may enforce that part of it which is enforceable under United Kingdom law — for example, the provisions for financial support of a spouse and children. The payee under a registered order may also request only partial enforcement of the order.

Generally speaking, orders of the Republic of Ireland are enforceable by the justices' clerk taking steps on his own initiative and in the same way as affiliation orders are enforceable. Payments are to be made through the justices' clerk, who shall remit them to the payee, or any named public authority in the Republic. (See r.10 of the Magistrates' Courts (Reciprocal Enforcement of Maintenance Orders) (Republic of Ireland) Rules 1975.) (S.I. 1975 No.286).

However, no sums accruing under an order before April 1 1975 shall be enforceable.

103. **Variation and revocation of maintenance orders made in the Republic of Ireland and registered in the United Kingdom. S.9 of the Act as modified.**

It must be noted that a United Kingdom Court *has no power whatsoever* to vary an order which has been made in the Republic of Ireland and which has subsequently been registered in a United Kingdom Court.

The applicant to vary should apply to the appropriate District Court in the Republic for the necessary form of application. The justices' clerk may be able to help the unrepresented applicant in obtaining such a form. The applicant should then submit the form together with a letter containing the particulars which form the basis of his application to the appropriate district court clerk. The law of the Republic of Ireland allows a letter of this nature to be admitted as evidence in support of the application.

If the order is varied in the Republic, the justices' clerk upon receiving the same shall register it in his court. (Rule 8). If the order is revoked, only the arrears, if any, which may have accrued between April 1 1975 and the date of revocation may then be enforced, and the registration shall cease to have effect as from the date of revocation.

At this juncture, it is worth noting that a court in the Irish Republic has no power to vary a United Kingdom maintenance order. A payer in the

Irish Republic wishing to apply to vary an order made in England or Wales will have to bring proceedings in the English or Welsh Court.

However, the payer's evidence in support of his application can be taken in the Irish Republic and this would be admissible in England and Wales under s.13 of the Act of 1972 (as modified by the 1974 order) (see para. 106 of this guide).

104. **Cancellation of registration of orders made in the Irish Republic and transfer thereof to other courts — s.10 of the Act of 1972 as mofidied.**

Subsection (1) of this section provides as follows:-

"Where a registered order is revoked by an order made by a court in the Republic of Ireland and notice of the revocation is received by the registering court, the prescribed officer of the registering court shall cancel the registration; but any arrears due under the registered order at the date on which the order of revocation took effect or April 1 1975, whichever is the later, shall continue to be recoverable as if the registration had not been cancelled".

The remaining subsections of this section remain unmodified in its application to the Irish Republic, and therefore, para. 57 ante relating to cancellation of overseas registered orders generally, apply, bearing in mind that only the Irish Republic courts can revoke their own orders.

105. **Appeals — s.12 of the Act of 1972 as modified.**

No appeal may lie against the making of a provisional order against a person residing in the Republic, but either party may appeal against the justices' decision to confirm, or refusal to confirm, a provisional order. A complainant may also appeal where justices refuse to make a provisional order in her favour.

106. **Admissibility of evidence taken in the Irish Republic. Ss. 13, 14, and 15 of the 1972 Act as modified.**

These sections allow for the admissibility in magistrates' courts in England and Wales of evidence taken in the Republic; proof of signatures to the documents not being required, and so on. Provision is also made for courts in England and Wales to request the authorities in the Republic to take any further evidence which may be required, but it should be noted that all such requests for further evidence must be transmitted to the courts in the Republic via the Secretary of State at the Home Office. Where a court in England or Wales receives from the Home Office a request to take further evidence from a person in any proceedings to which the Act applies for the purposes of a court hearing in the Republic, that person, unless he is the payer or the payee, is to be paid his witness expenses out of central funds.

All evidence taken in response to any such request from a court in the Irish Republic must be taken by way of signed and sworn deposition.

107. **Proceedings for maintenance orders originating in the Republic of Ireland.**

It would seem that proceedings commenced in the Republic of Ireland against a respondent residing in England and Wales can be pursued in a far less complicated way. The court in the Republic does not need to make, first, a provisional order, and then hold a second or "confirmation" hearing.

Rule 14 of the Magistrates' Courts (Reciprocal Enforcement of Maintenance Orders) (Republic of Ireland) Rules 1975 provides as follows:-

(1) Where the clerk of a magistrates' court receives from the Secretary of State a notice of the issue of the summons or other originating document in proceedings in the Republic of Ireland in relation to the making, variation or revocation of a maintenance order and it appears to that justices' clerk that the person against whom those proceedings have been instituted is residing within the petty sessions area for which the court acts, the justices' clerk shall serve the notice on that person by sending it by post in a registered letter addressed to him at his last known or usual place of abode.

(2) Where it appears to a justices' clerk who has received such a notice from the Secretary of State that the person against whom the proceedings have been instituted is not so residing, the justices' clerk shall send the notice to the Secretary of State.

(3) Where a justices' clerk serves a notice in pursuance of para.(1) above he shall send a document which establishes that the notice was so served to the Secretary of State for transmission to the responsible authority in the Republic of Ireland.

108. **Right of respondent resident in the United Kingdom to adduce evidence by way of affidavit in defence of proceedings in the Irish Republic.**

Where the respondent decides not to attend the hearing at the court in the Republic of Ireland, he may, by virtue of the Irish Republic's Maintenance Orders Act 1974, s.22(1)(c) swear an affidavit or other document before a Judge, magistrate, or officer of a court in the United Kingdom, and send this document to the court in the Irish Republic. The document may, without further proof, be admitted as evidence of any fact stated therein to the same extent as oral evidence of that fact would be admissible in those proceedings. The evidence of the Respondent's witnesses, if any can be dealt with in exactly the same way.

109. **Taking in England and Wales of further evidence for transmission to the Irish Republic.**

As indicated under the heading relating to s.13, 14 and 15 (para. 106 ante), magistrates' courts in England and Wales may receive requests from the courts in the Irish Republic for the taking of further evidence in connection with proceedings in those courts. Such evidence should be taken by way of signed and sworn depositions and transmitted to the Secretary of State for subsequent transmission, via the Master of the High Court in Dublin, to the appropriate district court in the Republic of Ireland.

THE HAGUE CONVENTION COUNTRIES

110. **The Reciprocal Enforcement of Maintenance Orders (Hague Convention Countries) Order 1979.**

At present, this Order applies to the following countries, namely:-
Czechoslovakia
Finland
France
Italy

Luxembourg
Netherlands (Kingdom in Europe and Netherlands Antilles)
Norway
Portugal
Sweden
Switzerland
Turkey

The order gives effect to the Convention on the Recognition and Enforcement of Decisions relating to Maintenance Obligations done at The Hague on 2nd October 1973.

It applies the provisions of Part I of the Maintenance Orders (Reciprocal Enforcement) Act 1972 to those countries, thus making them reciprocal countries under the Act, and therefore, the determination of the matter will be in accordance with (so far as England and Wales are concerned) the law of England and Wales.

The above countries, as well as being Hague Convention Countries, are also designated as Convention Countries under Part II of the Act (See Introduction to this Guide, and para. 35 ante).

The Home Office, in its circular number HOC 15/1980 dated February 26 1980 has this advice to offer, namely:-

"So far as proceedings initiated by a complainant in a Hague Convention Country are concerned, the documents received from the authorities in that country will indicate which procedure is being followed and will govern the manner in which the case is dealt with in this country. However, where a complainant in this country wishes to proceed against a defendant in a Hague Convention country, a choice will exist. Normally, courts will probably find it quicker and more straightforward to proceed under the new Hague Convention arrangements (that is, by making an order and transmitting it to the other country concerned for recognition and enforcement) than to rely on the earlier United Nations Convention arrangements (which entail the transmission of a claim for determination by a foreign court). There may, however, be some circumstances in which it could be to the complainant's advantage still to use the United Nations Convention, where, for example, leaving the order to be made in a country with a higher standard of living could lead to its being made for a higher amount than would be ordered in this country".

The order above mentioned applying to the Hague Convention countries modifies the original Part I of the Act of 1972, and the modified Part I is completely set out in sch. 3 to the Order. (S.I. 1979 No.1317). References to sections in this Part of this Guide, therefore, are references to the sections as so modified.

The procedure under the 1973 Hague Convention is, from a UK point of view, simply a slightly modified version of Part I of the 1972 Act. It should, however, be borne in mind that the legal systems of the other Hague Convention countries are very different from our own, and those involved should not be surprised if the action taken by the authorities in these countries does not follow the same pattern as that taken in commonwealth countries.

This is the second such modification of Part I of the main Act of 1972. The first such modification was made in applying the reciprocal provisions

to the Irish Republic, dealt with in the preceeding section of this Guide —
see paras. 91 to 109.

111. **Orders to be substantive orders and not provisional orders.**
Unlike the procedure in relation to other reciprocating countries
(including the Irish Republic) the orders made by courts in the United
Kingdom, applying the Hague Convention arrangements, will be
substantive orders rather than provisional orders, and will not, therefore,
require confirmation either abroad or by the court which made it.

112. **Definition of Maintenance Order.**
Section 21 of the Act of 1972 (as modified in its application to the
Hague Convention Countries) defines the term "Maintenance Order" as
meaning —
an order (however described), including a settlement made by or before
a competent court in a Hague Convention country, of any of the
following descriptions, and, in the case of an order which is not limited
to the following descriptions, the part of the order which is so limited,
that is to say:-

(a) an order (including an affiliation order or order consequent
upon an affiliation order) which provides for the periodical
payment of sums of money towards the maintenance of any
person, being a person whom the person liable to make payments
under the order is, according to the law applied in the place where
the order was made, liable to maintain;
　　(aa) an order which has been made in Scotland, on or after
　　the granting of a decree of divorce, for the payment of a
　　periodical allowance by one party to the marriage to the
　　other party;

(b) an affiliation order or order consequent upon an affiliation
order, being an order which provides for the payment by a person
adjudged, found or declared to be a child's father of expenses
incidental to the child's birth or, where the child has died, of his
funeral expenses; and

(c) an order within the foregoing provisions of this definition
made against a payer on the application of a public body which
claims reimbursement of sums of money payable under the order
with respect to the payee if reimbursement can be obtained by the
public body under the law to which it is subject,
and, in the case of a maintenance order which has been varied (including
a maintenance order which has been varied either by a court in the
United Kingdom or by a competent court in a Hague Convention
country whether or not the original order was made by such a court),
means that order as varied:
PROVIDED that the expression "maintenance order" shall not include
an order made in a Hague Convention country of a description which
that country or the United Kingdom has reserved the right under art.26
of the Hague Convention not to recognise or enforce;

113. **Transmission of maintenance order made in the United Kingdom for recognition and enforcement in a Hague Convention Country s.2 of the Act (as modified).**

This section provides as follows:-

(1) subject to subs. (2) below, where the payer under a maintenance order made, whether before, on or after 1st March 1980, by a court in the United Kingdom is residing in a Hague Convention country, the payee under the order may apply for the order to be sent to that country for recognition and enforcement.

(2) Subsection (1) above shall not have effect in relation to a maintenance order made under s.3 of this Act or to an order made by virtue of a provision of Part II of this Act.

(3) Every application under this section shall be made in the prescribed manner to the prescribed officer of the court which made the maintenance order to which the application relates.

(4) If, on an application duly made under this section to the prescribed officer of a court in the United Kingdom, that officer is satisfied that the payer under the maintenance order to which the application relates is residing in a Hague Convention country, the following documents, that is to say:-

(a) a certified copy of the maintenance order;

(b) a certificate signed by that officer certifying that the order is enforceable and that it is no longer subject to the ordinary forms of review;

(c) a certificate of arrears so signed;

(d) a statement giving such information as the officer possesses as to the whereabouts of the payer;

(e) a statement giving such information as the officer possesses for facilitating the identification of the payer;

(f) where available, a photograph of the payer;

(g) a written statement signed by that officer as to whether or not the payer appeared in the proceedings in which the maintenance order was made, and, if he did not appear, the original or a certified copy of a document which establishes that notice of the institution of the proceedings, including notice of the substance of the claim, was served on the payer;

(h) a document which establishes that notice of the order was sent to the payer; and

(i) a written statement signed by that officer as to whether or not the payee received legal aid either in the said proceedings or in connection with the said application;

shall be sent by that officer to the Secretary of State with a view to their being transmitted by the Secretary of State to the appropriate authority in the Hague Convention country if he is satisfied that the statement relating to the whereabouts of the payer gives sufficient information to justify that being done.

(5) Nothing in this section shall be taken as affecting any jurisdiction of a court in the United Kingdom with respect to a maintenance order to which this section applies, and subject to s.5 any such order may be enforced, varied or revoked accordingly.

Notes:

The Magistrates' Courts (Reciprocal Enforcement of Maintenance Orders) (Hague Convention Countries) Rules 1980 provide the machinery for the operation of the modified Part I in relation to the Hague Convention countries.

Rule 3 of the above mentioned Rules prescribe that the justices' clerk shall be the prescribed officer in relation to a magistrates' court.

Rule 4 sets out the steps to be taken by the payee to secure registration in accordance with the above quoted section. The procedure to be followed is the same as that set out in para. 92 hereof in relation to the Irish Republic.

A certificate of arrears includes a certificate to the effect that there are, in fact, no arrears owing. The certificate should not include any arrears accrued before the entry into force of the Hague Convention between the United Kingdom and the country addressed. So far as the countries mentioned in para.110 of this guide are concerned, the appropriate dates are as follows:-

Czechoslovakia 1/3/80, Finland 1/7/83, France 1/3/80, Italy 1/1/82, Luxembourg 1/6/81, Netherlands 1/3/81, Norway 1/3/80, Portugal 1/3/80, Sweden 1/3/80, Switzerland 1/3/80, and Turkey 1/11/83.

Clerks to justices should refer to the Home Office circular accompanying the relevant designation order to discover the operative date of arrangements with any particular country which may in the future become a signatory to the Hague Convention.

A certificate that the order is no longer subject to the ordinary forms of review may be given after the time limit for appeal has expired. In issuing the certificate no account should be taken of the fact that a perogative writ may still be applied for, unless, of course, the justices' clerk has been served with Notice of Motion to that effect, or, depending on the circumstances, has information to the effect that application for such writ is definitely being considered.

This section contemplates that a full substantive order was made while the parties were both resident in the United Kingdom, and that the payer subsequently moved to one of the Hague Convention countries. It will be observed that an order made in the United Kingdom under the "Convention" provisions cannot be transmitted under this section for enforcement. (The "Convention" provisions are set out in paras. 61 to 90 (inclusive) in this Guide and deal with Part II of the Maintenance Orders (Reciprocal Enforcement) Act 1972).

The position where the payer moves to, or is residing in, a Hague Convention country before an order is made is dealt with in the next section — s.3 (para. 114 of this guide).

An application for transmission of an order under s.2 should be made to the appropriate officer of the court which made the order, for example, the justices' clerk of the magistrates' court, or, if the order was made in the county court, to the registrar of that court.

114. **Power of magistrates' court to make a maintenance order against a person residing in a Hague Convention country — s.3 of the Act (as modified)**

This section, which applies only to magistrates' courts, provides as follows:-

(1) Where a complaint is made to a magistrates' court by a person who is habitually resident in England and Wales against a person residing in a Hague Convention country and the complaint is one on which the court

would have jurisdiction by virtue of any enactment to make a maintenance order if at the time when the proceedings were instituted —

(a) the defendant were residing in England and Wales; and

(b) a summons to appear before the court to answer to the complaint had been duly served on him,

the court shall have jurisdiction to hear the complaint and may subject to the following provisions of this section make a maintenance order on the complaint.

(3) If the court hearing a complaint to which subsection (1) above applies is satisfied —

(a) that there are grounds on which a maintenance order containing a provision requiring the making of payments for the maintenance of a child may be made on that complaint, but

(b) that it has no jurisdiction to make that order unless it also makes an order providing for the legal custody of that child,

then, for the purpose of enabling the court to make the maintenance order, the complainant shall be deemed to be the person to whom the legal custody of that child has been committed by an order of the court which is for the time being in force.

(4) No enactment empowering a magistrates' court to refuse to make an order on a complaint on the ground that the matter in question is one which would be more conveniently dealt with by the High Court shall apply in relation to a complaint to which subs. (1) above applies.

(5) On the making of a complaint to which subs. (1) applies, the following documents, that is to say:-

(a) notice of the institution of the proceedings, including notice of the substance of the complaint; (form 17)

(b) a statement, signed by the prescribed officer of the court, giving such information as he possesses as to the whereabouts of the defendant;

(c) a statement giving such information as the officer possesses for facilitating the identification of the defendant; and

(d) where available, a photograph of the defendant;

shall be sent by that officer to the Secretary of State with a view to their being transmitted by the Secretary of State to the appropriate authority in the Hague Convention country in which the defendant is residing for service on him of the document mentioned in para. (a) above if he is satisfied that the statement relating to the whereabouts of the defendant gives sufficient information to justify that being done.

(6) In considering whether or not to make a maintenance order pursuant to a complaint to which subs. (1) above applies the court shall take into account any representations made and any evidence adduced by or on behalf of the defendant.

(6A) Where the defendant makes any representations or adduces any evidence, a copy of the representations or evidence shall be served on the complainant by the prescribed officer of the court before the hearing.

(6B) The prescribed officer of the court shall give the defendant notice in writing of the date fixed for the hearing by sending the notice by post addressed to his last known or usual place of abode.

(6C) A maintenance order pursuant to a complaint in which subs.(1)

62

above applies shall not be made unless the document mentioned in subs. (5)(a) above has been served on the defendant in accordance with the law for the service of such documents in the Hague Convention country in which he is residing or in such other manner as may be authorised by the Secretary of State not less than six weeks previously.

(6D) Where a maintenance order has been made under this Section, the prescribed officer of the court shall send the following documents, that is to say:-

      (a) a certified copy of the order;

      (b) a certificate signed by that officer certifying that the order is enforceable and that it is no longer subject to the ordinary forms of review;

      (c) a written statement signed by that officer as to whether or not the defendant appeared in the proceedings in which the order was made, and, if he did not appear, the original or a certified copy of a document which esablishes that the document mentioned in subs. (5)(a) above has been served on the payer in accordance with subs. (6C) above;

      (d) a document which establishes that notice of the order was sent to the defendant; and

      (e) a written statement signed by that officer as to whether or not the complainant received legal aid in the proceedings;

to the Secretary of State with a view to their being transmitted by the Secretary of State to the appropriate authority in the Hague Convention country in which the defendant resides for recognition and enforcement of the order.

(6E) A maintenance order made under this section may, subject to s.5 of this Act be enforced, varied or revoked in like manner as any other maintenance order made by a magistrates' court.

(7) In the application of this section to Northern Ireland, in subs. (1) for the reference to England and Wales there shall be substituted a reference to Northern Ireland and in subs. (4) for the reference to the High Court there shall be substituted a reference to the High Court of Justice in Northern Ireland.

Notes

Subsection (5)(a) requires a notice of institution of proceedings to be prepared (see form No.17). It is submitted that the term "substance of the complaint" means not only the ground(s) upon which the order is being sought, but particulars of the allegations which the complainant intends to adduce in evidence in support of the complaint.

In subs. 6D(c), a certificate of non-appearance would be given if the defendant ignored the proceedings altogether. He would be deemed to have appeared if he sent sworn evidence by way of deposition or affidavit in defence of the proceedings, or if he sent written representations as to the amount of the order. Note the magistrates' court's power under s.14(5) — see para. 123 — to make a request via the Secretary of State for further evidence if the court considers it necessary. The defendant would, of course, be entitled to appear in person and/or by legal representative to contest the proceedings.

Section 6D (b) and (d) — Notice of the making of the order should be sent forthwith to the defendant. A certified copy of the order would probably suffice. It will not be possible to send the papers to the Secretary of State until at least 21 days have elapsed to enable the time limit for an appeal to expire. See the note under s.2 in para. 113 insofar as prerogative writs are concerned.

115. **Variation and revocation of maintenance order made in the United Kingdom — s.5 of the Act (as modified).**

(1) This section applies to a maintenance order a certified copy of which has been sent to a Hague Convention country for recognition and enforcement of the order.

(2) The jurisdiction of a magistrates' court to revoke or vary a maintenance order shall be exerciseable notwithstanding that the proceedings for the revocation or variation, as the case may be, of the order are brought by or against a person residing in a Hague Convention country.

(3) Where an application is made by the payee to a court in England and Wales or Northern Ireland for the variation or revocation of an order to which this section applies, and the payer is residing in a Hague Convention country, the prescribed officer of the court shall send to the Secretary of State notice of the institution of the proceedings, including notice of the substance of the application, with a view to it being transmitted to the appropriate authority in the Hague Convention country for service on the payer.

(4) Where an application is made by the payee to a court in England and Wales or Northern Ireland for the variation or revocation of an order to which this section applies, and the payer is residing in a Hague Convention country —

(a) the court, in considering whether or not to vary or revoke the order, shall take into account any representations made and any evidence adduced by or on behalf of the payer;

(b) a copy of any such representations or evidence shall be served on the payee in the prescribed manner before the hearing;

(c) the prescribed officer of the court shall give the payer notice in writing of the date fixed for the hearing by sending the notice by post addressed to his last known or usual place of abode. (See form 18).

(5) Where an application is made by the payee to a court in England and Wales or Northern Ireland for the variation or revocation of an order to which this section applies, and the payer is residing in a Hague Convention country, the order shall not be varied or revoked unless the document mentioned in subs. (3) above has been served on the payer in accordance with the law for the service of such a document in the Hague Convention country not less than six weeks previously.

(6) Where an application is made by the payer to a court in England and Wales or Northern Ireland for the variation or revocation of an order to which this section applies, the prescribed officer of the court shall arrange for the service of the document mentioned in subs. (3) above on the payee.

(7) Where an order to which this section applies is varied or revoked by a court in the United Kingdom the prescribed officer of the court shall

send the following documents, that is to say:-

(a) a certified copy of the order of variation or revocation;

(b) a certificate signed by that officer certifying that the order of variation or revocation is enforceable and that it is no longer subject to the ordinary forms of review;

(c) a written statement, signed by that officer as to whether or not the defendant or, in Scotland, the defender, appeared in the proceedings for the variation or revocation of the order, and if he did not appear, the original or a certified copy of a document which establishes that notice of the institution of the proceedings has been served on the defendant, or, as the case may be, the defender;

(d) a document which establishes that notice of the order of variation or revocation was sent to the defendant; and

(e) a written statement signed by that officer as to whether or not the payer or the payee received legal aid in the proceedings;

to the Secretary of State with a view to their being transmitted by the Secretary of State to the appropriate authority in the Hague Convention country for recognition and enforcement of the order of variation or revocation.

(8) Where a maintenance order to which this section applies has been varied by an order made by a court in the United Kingdom or by a competent court in a Hague Convention country the maintenance order shall, as from the date on which the order of variation took effect, have effect as varied by that order.

(9) Where a maintenance order to which this section applies has been revoked by an order made by a court in the United Kingdom or by a competent court in a Hague Convention country the maintenance order shall, as from the date on which the order of revocation took effect, be deemed to have ceased to have effect except as respects any arrears due under the maintenance order at that date.

(10) Where a maintenance order to which this section applies has been varied or revoked by an order made by a competent court in a Hague Convention country, the prescribed officer of the court shall register the order of variation or revocation in the prescribed manner.

Notes

The Magistrates' Courts (Reciprocal Enforcement of Maintenance Orders) (Hague Convention Countries) Rules 1980 — r.6 — provides that a copy of any representations made or evidence adduced under s.5(4)(b) above by or on behalf of the payer in an application by the payee for the variation or revocation of a maintenance order to which s.5 applies, shall be sent to the payee by post by the justices' clerk.

Rule 5 of the same Rules provides that the order shall be registered by means of a signed minute or memorandum in the court register. The entry must be signed by the justices' clerk. The minute or memorandum must specify the Act and section under which the order is registered.

It will be noted that orders made by the courts in the United Kingdom can be varied by the court in the United Kingdom and by the court in the Hague Convention country. Concurrent jurisdiction to vary exists.

Application to the United Kingdom court for variation of the order should be made to the court which made the original order. For example, where a county court order has been transmitted under s.2 for recognition and enforcement, application should be made to the county court to vary it.

Written notice of all registrations under this Act shall be sent to the Secretary of State (r.5(3) of the above cited Rules).

For procedure applicable upon application to vary an order made in a Hague Convention country and registered in a magistrates' court in England and Wales, see s.9 of the (modified) Part I of the Act of 1972 (para. 119 of this Guide).

116. **Registration in United Kingdom court of maintenance order made In Hague Convention country — s.6 of the Act (as modified).**

(1) This section applies to a maintenance order made whether before or on or after March 1 1980 by a competent court in a Hague Convention country.

(2) Where a certified copy of an order to which this section applies is received by the Secretary of State from a Hague Convention country, and it appears to the Secretary of State that the payer under the order is residing in the United Kingdom, he shall send the copy of the order and the accompanying documents to the prescribed officer of the appropriate court.

(3) Where the prescribed officer of the appropriate court receives from the Secretary of State a certified copy of an order to which this section applies, he shall, subject to the following subsections, register the order in the prescribed manner in that court.

(4) Before registering an order under this section an officer of a court shall take such steps as he thinks fit for the purpose of ascertaining whether the payer under the order is residing within the jurisdiction of the court, and if after taking those steps he is satisfied that the payer is not so residing he shall return the certified copy of the order and the accompanying documents to the Secretary of State with a statement giving such information as he possesses as to the whereabouts of the payer.

(5) (a) The prescribed officer of the appropriate court may refuse to authorise the registration of the order if the court in the Hague Convention country by or before which the order was made did not have jurisdiction to make the order; and for these purposes a court in a Hague Convention country shall be considered to have jurisdiction if—

(i) either the payer or the payee had his habitual residence in the Hague Convention country at the time when the proceedings were instituted; or

(ii) the payer and the payee were nationals of that country at that time; or

(iii) the defendant in those proceedings had submitted to the jurisdiction of the court, either expressly or by defending on the merits of the case without objecting to the jurisdiction; or

(iv) in the case of an order made by reason of a divorce or a legal separation or a declaration that a marriage is void or annulled, the court is recognised by the law of the part of the United Kingdom in which enforcement is sought as having jurisdiction to make the order.

(b) In deciding whether a court in a Hague Convention country had jurisdiction to make an order the prescribed officer shall be bound by any finding of fact on which the court based its jurisdiction.

(6) The prescribed officer of the appropriate court may refuse to authorise the registration of the order —

(a) if such registration is manifestly contrary to public policy;

(b) if the order was obtained by fraud in connection with a matter of procedure;

(c) if proceedings between the same parties and having the same purpose are pending before a court in the same part of the United Kingdom and those proceedings were the first to be instituted; or

(d) if the order is incompatible with an order made in proceedings between the same parties and having the same purpose, either in the United Kingdom or in another country, provided that the latter order itself fulfils the conditions necessary for its registration and enforcement under this Part of this Act.

(7) Without prejudice to subs. (6) above, if the payer did not appear in the proceedings in the Hague Convention country in which the order was made, the prescribed officer of the appropriate court shall refuse to authorise the registration of the order unless notice of the institution of the proceedings, including notice of the substance of the claim, was served on the payer in accordance with the law of that Hague Convention country and if, having regard to the circumstances, the payer had sufficient time to enable him to defend the proceedings.

(8) If the order is registered under subs. (3) above, the prescribed officer of the appropriate court shall serve notice in a prescribed form on the payer and give notice to the payee that the order has been registered.

(9) The payer may, within one calendar month from the date of service of the said notice, appeal to the court in which the order is registered to set aside the registration of the order on one of the grounds set out in paras. (5), (6) and (7) above.

(10) If the payer appeals to the court in which the order is registered to set aside the registration of the order, the prescribed officer of the court shall give notice to the payee of the appeal and of the date of the hearing of the appeal.

(11) If the prescribed officer refuses to register the order, he shall give notice to the payee in a prescribed form that registration has been refused.

(12) A payee to whom notice has been given by the prescribed officer of any court under subs. (11) above may within one calendar month from the date when the notice was given, appeal to that court against the refusal to register the order.

(13) If the payee appeals to the court against the refusal to register the order, the prescribed officer of the court shall give notice to the payer of the appeal and of the date of the hearing of the appeal.

Notes

On the question of registration and appeal against the refusal to register, or appeal against registration, see paras. 98, 99 and 100 of this Guide dealing with the application of the Act to the Irish Republic.

However, it should be borne in mind that in Hague Convention Cases, the magistrates' court lacks the power to stay the proceedings upon an appeal being lodged by the payer against registration as described in para. 99 in Irish cases. Note the decision in Armitage v Nanchen quoted in para. 98 of this Guide concerning public policy in connexion with the reciprocal recovery of maintenance.

See form 19 for prescribed form of notice to payer of the registration of the order, and form 20 for the prescribed form of notice to the payee of non-registration. The prescribed notice of appeal by the payee against non-registration is shown at form 21.

117. **Application of rules concerning notice in regard to registered orders and payments to be made under such orders.**

The Magistrates' Courts (Reciprocal Enforcement of Maintenance Orders) (Hague Convention countries) Rules 1980 — and, in particular, r.7 and 8 provide, respectively, as follows:-

7. (1) Any notice required under s.6(8) of the Act (notice of registration in United Kingdom court of maintenance order made in Hague Convention country) to be served on the payer under a maintenance order shall, where the order is registered in a magistrates' court, be in the form in Part I of sch.2 to these Rules, or in a form to the like effect.

(2) Where a magistrates' court to which an appeal is made under s.6(9) of the Act sets aside the registration of the order, the justices' clerk shall send written notice of the court's decision to the Secretary of State.

(3) Any notice required under s.6 (11) of the Act (notice that maintenance order made in Hague Convention country has not been registered in United Kingdom court) to be given to the payee under a maintenance order shall, where the appropriate court is a magistrates' court, be in the form in Part II of sch.2 to these Rules or in a form to the like effect.

8 (1) Payment of sums due under a registered order shall, while the order is registered in a magistrates' court, be made to the clerk of the registering court during such hours and at such place as that clerk may direct; and a justices' clerk to whom payments are made shall send those payments by post to the payee under the order.

(2) Where it appears to a justices' clerk to whom payments under any maintenance order are to be made by virtue of para. (1) above that any sums payable under the order are in arrear he may and, if such sums are in arrear to an amount equal to four times the sum payable weekly under the order, he shall, whether the person for whose benefit the payment should have been made requests him to do so or not, proceed in his own name for the recovery of those sums, unless it appears to him that it is unreasonable in the circumstances to do so.

118. **Enforcement of maintenance orders registered in United Kingdom Court — s.8 of the Act of 1972 (as modified).**

No arrears which have accrued before the appropriate date shown in para. 113 of this Guide may be enforced.

The order is to be enforced as if it were an order of a magistrates' court, and as if it were an affiliation order. The provisions relating to the enforcement of orders made in the Irish Republic and registered in England and Wales are almost identical to the provisions relating to the enforcement of Hague Convention orders. See, therefore, para.102 relating to the Irish Republic.

Note the obligation placed upon the justices' clerk to enforce the order and the arrears, contained in r.8(2) as set out in the preceeding paragraph.

119. **Variation of maintenance order registered in United Kingdom court — s.9 of the Act of 1972 (as modified).**

(1) Subject to the provisions of this section:-

(a) the registering court shall have the like power, on an application made by the payer or payee under a registered order, to vary the order as if it had been made by the registering court and as if that court had had jurisdiction to make it;

(b) the jurisdiction of a magistrates' court to vary a registered order shall be exercisable notwithstanding that the proceedings for the variation of the order are brought by or against a person residing in a Hague Convention country.

(2) The registering court shall not vary a registered order unless —

(a) the payer under the order had his habitual residence in the United Kingdom at the time when the proceedings to vary the order were instituted; or

(b) the defendant in those proceedings had submitted to the jurisdiction of the registering court either expressly or by defending on the merits of the case without objecting to the jurisdiction.

(3) Where an application is made to a registering court in England and Wales or Northern Ireland by the payer for the variation of a registered order, and the payee is residing in a Hague Convention country, the prescribed officer of the court shall send to the Secretary of State notice of the institution of the proceedings, including notice of the substance of the application, with a view to it being transmitted to the appropriate authority in the Hague Convention country for service on the payee.

(4) Where an application is made by the payer to a registering court in England and Wales or Northern Ireland for the variation of a registered order —

(a) the court, in considering whether or not to vary the order, shall take into account any representations made and any evidence adduced by or on behalf of the payee;

(b) a copy of any such representations and evidence shall be served on the payer by the prescribed officer of the court before the hearing;

(c) the prescribed officer of the court shall give the payee notice in writing of the date fixed for the hearing by sending the notice by post addressed to his last known or usual place of abode.

(5) Where an application is made by the payer to a registering court in England and Wales or Northern Ireland for the variation of a registered order and the payee is residing in a Hague Convention country, the order shall not be varied unless the document mentioned in subs. (3) above has been served on the payee in accordance with the law for the

service of such a document in the Hague Convention country not less than six weeks previously.

(6) Where an application is made by the payee to a registering Court in England and Wales or Northern Ireland for the variation of a registered order, the prescribed officer of the court shall serve the document mentioned in subs. (3) above on the payer.

(7) Where a registered order is varied by a registering court in the United Kingdom the prescribed officer of the court shall send the following documents, that is to say:-

    (a) a certified copy of the order of variation;

    (b) a certificate signed by that officer certifying that the order of variation is enforceable and that it is no longer subject to the ordinary forms of review;

    (c) a written statement signed by that officer as to whether or not the defendant or, in Scotland, the defender appeared in the proceedings for the variation of the order, and, if he did not appear, the original or a certified copy of a document which establishes that notice of the institution of the proceedings has been served on the defendant or, as the case may be, the defender; and

    (d) a written statement signed by that officer as to whether or not the payer or the payee received legal aid in the proceedings

to the Secretary of State with a view to their being transmitted by the Secretary of State to the appropriate authority in the Hague Convention country for recognition and enforcement of the order of variation.

(8) Where a registered order has been varied by the registering court or by a court in a Hague Convention country, the prescribed officer of the registering court shall register the variation order in the prescribed manner.

(9) Where a registered order has been varied by the registering court or by a court in a Hague Convention country, the registered order shall, as from the date on which the variation took effect have effect as so varied.

Notes

As to notice of institution of proceedings, form 17 to this Guide may be adapted.

Note the lack of jurisdiction of the *Registering* court to *revoke* an order made in a Hague Convention country. The notes to s.3 written at para.114 apply equally to this section.

120. **Cancellation of registration and transfer of order — s.10 of the Act of 1972 (as modified).**

    (1) Where a registered order is revoked by an order made by a court in a Hague Convention country and notice of the revocation is received by the registering court, the prescribed officer of the registering court shall cancel the registration, but any arrears due under the registered order at the date on which the order of revocation took effect, other than, in the case of a registered order made by a court in a Hague Convention country prior to the date of the entry into force of the Hague Convention between the United Kingdom and that country, arrears due before that date, shall continue to be recoverable as if the registration had not been

cancelled.

(2) Where the prescribed officer of the registering court is of opinion that the payer under a registered order has ceased to reside within the jurisdiction of that court, he shall cancel the registration of the order and, subject to subs. (3) below, shall send the certified copy of the order to the Secretary of State.

(3) Where the prescribed officer of the registering court, being a magistrates' court, is of opinion that the payer is residing within the jurisdiction of another magistrates' court in that part of the United Kingdom in which the registering court is, he shall transfer the order to that other court by sending the certified copy of the order to the prescribed officer of that other court.

(4) On the transfer of an order under subs. (3) above the prescribed officer of the court to which it is transferred shall, subject to subs. (6) below, register the order in the prescribed manner in that court.

(5) Where the certified copy of an order is received by the Secretary of State under this section and it appears to him that the payer under the order is still residing in the United Kingdom, he shall transfer the order to the appropriate court by sending the certified copy of the order together with the related documents to the prescribed officer of the appropriate court, and subject to subs.(6) below, that officer shall register the order in the prescribed manner in that court.

(6) Before registering an order in pursuance of subs. (4) or (5) above an officer of a court shall take such steps as he thinks fit for the purpose of ascertaining whether the payer is residing within the jurisdiction of the court, and if after taking those steps he is satisfied that the payer is not so residing he shall send the certified copy of the order to the Secretary of State.

(7) The officer of a court who is required by any of the foregoing provisions of this section to send to the Secretary of State or to the prescribed officer of another court the certified copy of an order shall send with that copy —

(a) a certificate of arrears signed by him;

(b) a statement giving such information as he possesses as to the whereabouts of the payer; and

(c) any relevant documents in his possession relating to the case.

Notes

See para. 57 (ante) which deals with cancellation and transfer of registered orders in the un-modified form affecting reciprocating countries generally (excluding the Hague Convention countries and the Irish Republic).

See the next para. (para. 121 post) as to the duties of the justices' clerk following cancellation and re-registration of orders.

121. **Duty of justices' clerk following registration, or cancellation of registration, of order.**

Rule 10 of the Magistrates' Courts (Reciprocal Enforcement of Maintenance Orders) (Hague Convention Countries) Rules 1980 provides:-

(1) Where a justices' clerk cancels the registration of a maintenance

order under s.10(1) of the Act (cancellation of registration and transfer of order) he shall send written notice of the cancellation to the payer under the order.

(2) Where a justices' clerk registers a maintenance order under s.10(4) of the Act, he shall send written notice to the Secretary of State and to the payer under the order that the order has been duly registered.

122. **Appeals — s.12 of the Act (as modified).**

Provision is made for a like right of appeal by either party against the making or refusal to make a variation order under s.9 as such party would have had if the registered order had been made by the registering court.

123. **Admissibility of evidence taken in Hague Convention countries — ss.13, 14 and 15.**

These sections allow for the admissibility in the United Kingdom courts of evidence taken in the Hague Convention countries, the obtaining of evidence needed by a court in those countries, or in the United Kingdom, and the fact that signatures on the documents transmitted from abroad need not be proved at the proceedings.

The notes written at para. 106 (ante) in the application of the Act to the Irish Republic apply equally to the Hague Convention countries.

124. **Payments under Hague Convention orders and conversion to sterling — s.16 of the Act of 1972 (as modified) and Rule 8 of the 1980 Rules.**

Payments under Orders made in Hague Convention countries and registered in magistrates' courts in England and Wales are to be made through the justices' clerk. The amount of the order is to be converted into United Kingdom currency at the rate prevailing on the day when the order is registered. A certificate of arrears must be similarly converted.

125. **Justices' clerk to notify Secretary of State of service of notice.**

Rule 11 of the Magistrates' Courts (Reciprocal Enforcement of Maintenance Orders)(Hague Convention Countries) Rules 1980 provides as follows:-

"Where a justices' clerk serves a notice on a payer under a maintenance order who resides in a Hague Convention country under any provision of Part I of the Act, he shall send a document which establishes that the notice was so served to the Secretary of State"·

126. **Proceedings originating in a Hague Convention country and which are to be determined in that country.**

Rule 12 of the above cited Rules of 1980 provides as follows:-

(1) Where the clerk of a magistrates' court receives from the Secretary of State notice of the institution of proceedings, including notice of the substance of the claim, in a Hague Convention country in relation to the making, variation or revocation of a maintenance order and it appears to the justices' clerk that the person against whom those proceedings have been instituted is residing within the petty sessions area for which the court acts, the justices' clerk shall serve the notice on that person by sending it by post in a registered letter addressed to him at his last known or usual place of abode.

(2) Where it appears to a justices' clerk who has received such a notice from the Secretary of State that the person against whom the proceedings have been instituted is not so residing, the justices' clerk shall return the notice to the Secretary of State with an intimation to that effect.

127. Recording of Evidence

Where one party chooses to defend a complaint by means of sworn affidavit, or deposition, it is important that all evidence taken in the proceedings in England and Wales affecting the Hague Convention countries be by way of signed and sworn deposition, so that if the need arises for a request to be made for the taking of further evidence in a Hague Convention country, the original (or a certified copy) of the depositions can be transmitted with such a request.

In any event, a full note must be taken in the event of an appeal against the making, or refusal to make, an Order on the complaint.

128.   The Hague convention arrangements have been described in detail in this Guide in the preceding paras. 110 to 127. However, Magistrates clerks and practitioners may wish to know that outgoing Hague Convention cases can run into considerable problems, because of the different approach to the Convention taken by different countries. In particular, unlike the United Nations Convention (appendix "C" of this guide, and paras. 61 to 90) the Hague Convention provides no procedural machinery for handling these cases. As a result, the authorities in some countries will not accept Hague cases transmitted to them by the Home Office but argue that the applicant here must obtain the services of a lawyer in the country concerned to act on her behalf in placing the order before a court for recognition and enforcement. In appropriate cases, therefore, consideration should be given to using the United Nations Convention.

PAYEE MOVING OVERSEAS FOLLOWING MAKING OF ORDER IN UNITED KINGDOM

129.   The reciprocal provisions described in this guide are not designed to cover this situation.

At one time, the payer under an order was at a disadvantage when the payee subsequently moved overseas after having obtained a maintenance order in England and Wales.

Even after moving overseas, the payee could instruct the justices' clerk to enforce the order (and still can do so). She can also apply to the court to increase the order. However, the payer under the order had no remedy available to him which would enable him to apply for a reduction as a summons could not be served on the payee because she was outside the United Kingdom. Because of this obvious injustice, the law was subsequently altered in order to provide a remedy for the payer.

The position is now covered by s.24 of the Domestic Proceedings and Magistrates' Courts Act 1978, in husband and wife cases, and by s.41 of the Maintenance Orders (Reciprocal Enforcement) Act 1972 insofar as affiliation and Guardianship of Minors Acts orders are concerned. See also r.106 of the Magistrates' Courts Rules 1981.

It should be noted that the magistrates' court has no power to *increase* the amount of the order unless both parties are present or legally represented, or, if the payee is living in Scotland or Northern Ireland, a summons has been duly served on her, and she fails to respond thereto.

An important matter to be borne in mind is that where a High Court or County Court order has been registered in a magistrates' court under the Maintenance Orders Act 1958, the magistrates' court cannot entertain an application to vary the rate of payments under the order by virtue of s.4 of the said Act of 1958 unless both parties to the order are present in England and Wales. If, for example, the wife, whose order has been registered in a magistrates' court, goes to reside anywhere outside England or Wales, and the husband wishes to apply for a decreased order, he will have to go back to the county court, if that court made the order, to seek his remedy.

APPENDIX "A"

Countries and Territories to which the Maintenance Orders (Facilities for Enforcement) Act 1920 applies.

Note A provisional affiliation order cannot be made for transmission to any of the following countries or territories, nor may an existing affiliation order be transmitted for recognition and enforcement.

Country or Territory	Payments to be sent by justices' clerk to:-	Deletions (1972 Act applied as from:-
ANTIGUA	Crown agents	
BOTSWANA	do	
BAHAMAS	do	
BRITISH HONDURAS	do	
BRUNEI	do	
CAYMAN ISLANDS	do	
CYPRUS	do	
COCOS-KEELING ISLANDS	Overseas Court	
CHRISTMAS ISLAND	do	
DOMINICA	Crown Agents	
GAMBIA	do	
GUYANA	do	
GRENADA	Crown Agents	
GILBERT & ELLICE ISLANDS	do	
GUERNSEY	Overseas Court	
JAMAICA	Overseas Court	
JERSEY	Overseas Court	
LESOTHO	Crown Agents	
MALAWI	Crown Agents	
MAURITIUS	do	
MONTSERRAT	do	
MALAYSIA	do	
NIGERIA	do	

NEWFOUNDLAND	
(Canada)	Overseas Court
NEVIS	Crown Agents
PRICE EDWARD ISLAND	
(Canada)	Overseas Court
ST. CHRISTOPHER	Crown Agents
ST. LUCIA	Crown Agents
ST. VINCENT	Crown Agents
SEYCHELLES	Crown Agents
SOLOMON ISLANDS	Crown Agents
SIERRA LEONE	Crown Agents
SRI LANKA	Crown Agents
SOMALILAND	Crown Agents
SWAZILAND	Crown Agents
TRINIDAD AND TOBAGO	Crown Agents
UGANDA	Crown Agents
VIRGIN ISLANDS	Crown Agents
YUKON (Canada)	Overseas Court
ZANZIBAR	Crown Agents
ZAMBIA	Crown Agents

APPENDIX "B"

Countries and Territories to which Part I of the Maintenance Orders (Reciprocal Enforcement) Act 1972 applies.

RECIPROCATING COUNTRIES

Unless specifically excluded in Column 2 in the following Schedule, each of the countries or territories named will accept maintenance orders of all descriptions.

DESCRIPTION OF MAINTENANCE ORDER

CODE

—A— Provisional Affiliation Orders.
—AA— Affiliation Orders.
—B— An Affiliation Order or Order consequent upon an Affiliation Order, being an order which provides for the payment by a person adjudged, found or declared to be a child's father of expenses incidental to the child's birth, or where the child has died, of his funeral expenses.
—C— Order obtained by or in favour of a public authority.

Country or Territory	Maintenance Orders generally, except:	Provisional Variation Orders/Further evidence taken at request of Overseas Court to be sent to:		Can U.K. Provisional Variation Order be confirmed in Reciprocating Country? If no, power to vary absolutely	Payments collected by Justices' Clerk to be sent, unless otherwise directed by Home Office to:	
		Home Office	Direct to Overseas Court		Crown Agents	Direct to Overseas Court
AUSTRALIAN STATES						
CAPITAL TERRITORY	C		Yes	Yes		Yes
NEW SOUTH WALES	C		Yes	Yes		Yes
NORTHERN TERRITORY	C		Yes	Yes		Yes
SOUTH AUSTRALIA	C		Yes	Yes		Yes
TASMANIA	C		Yes	Yes		Yes
QUEENSLAND	C		Yes	Yes		Yes
VICTORIA	C		Yes	Yes		Yes
WESTERN AUSTRALIA	C		Yes	Yes		Yes
ANGUILLA	—		Yes	Yes	Yes	
BARBADOS	—		Yes	Yes	Yes	
BERMUDA	—		Yes	Yes	Yes	
CZECHOSLOVAKIA	See separate section dealing with Hague Convention Countries					
CANADIAN PROVINCES						
ALBERTA	A, B and C	Yes		No		Yes
BRITISH COLUMBIA	—	Yes		No		Yes
MANITOBA	—		Yes	Yes		Yes
NOVA SCOTIA	B and C	Yes		No		Yes
ONTARIO	B	Yes		No		Yes
NEW BRUNSWICK	AA, B and C	Yes		No		Yes
NORTH-WEST TERRITORIES	AA, B and C	Yes		No		Yes
SASKATCHEWAN	A and B	Yes		No		Yes
EIRE	See separate section re modified Part I and special procedure applicable to Irish Republic.					
FALKLAND ISLANDS AND DEPENDENCIES	—		Yes	Yes	Yes	
FRANCE	See separate section dealing with Hague Convention Countries.					
FIJI	—		Yes	Yes	Yes	
FINLAND	See separate section dealing with Hague Convention Countries.					
GHANA	AA and B	Yes		No	Yes	
GIBRALTAR	—		Yes	Yes	Yes	
HONG KONG	—		Yes	Yes	Yes	
INDIA	AA, B and C	Yes		No		Yes
ISLE OF MAN	—		Yes	Yes		Yes
ITALY	See separate section dealing with Hague Convention Countries					
LUXEMBOURG	See separate section dealing with Hague Convention Countries					
KENYA	AA and B	Yes		No	Yes	
MALTA	—		Yes	Yes		Yes
NAURU	—		Yes	Yes		Yes
NETHERLANDS	See separate section dealing with Hague Convention Countries					
NORWAY	See separate section dealing with Hague Convention Countries					
NEW ZEALAND	—	Yes		Yes		Yes
NORFOLK ISLAND	C		Yes	Yes		Yes
PAPUA NEW GUINEA	A	Yes		Yes		Yes
PORTUGAL	See separate section dealing with Hague Convention Countries					
ST. HELENA	—		Yes	Yes	Yes	
SINGAPORE	—		Yes	Yes	Yes	
SOUTH AFRICA (Republic of)	AA and B	Yes		No		Yes
SWEDEN	See separate section dealing with Hague Convention Countries					
SWITZERLAND	See separate section dealing with Hague Convention Countries					
TURKEY	See separate section dealing with Hague Convention Countries					
TURKS AND CAICOS ISLANDS	AA, B and C	Yes		No		Yes
TANZANIA (except Zanzibar)	AA, B and C	Yes		No	Yes	
ZIMBABWE	AA and B	Yes		No		Yes

ADDITIONS

NOTES TO APPENDIX "B"

It should be noted from Appendix "B" that some Countries exclude "AFFILIATION ORDERS" (described as Category "AA" in the appendix) while others exclude only "PROVISIONAL AFFILIATION ORDERS" (described as Category "A").

The Author takes the view that where Category "AA" (Affiliation Orders) is excluded by Column 2 of the Appendix, this also, by definition, excludes Provisional Affiliation Orders (Category "A") and, therefore, neither Sections 2 nor 3 of the Maintenance Orders (Reciprocal Enforcement) Act 1972 (paragraphs 37 and 39 of this Guide) can apply to those Countries insofar as Affiliation Orders (whether Provisional or Substantive) are concerned.

On the other hand, where only PROVISIONAL AFFILIATION ORDERS (Category "A") are expressly excluded by Column 2, it is open to a Payee who has already obtained an Affiliation Order in the United Kingdom to apply for that Order to be transmitted to the appropriate reciprocating Country under Section 2 of the Maintenance Orders (Reciprocal Enforcement) Act 1972 (Paragraph 37 of this Guide) for recognition and enforcement.

To take the Canadian Provinces as an example:-

BRITISH COLUMBIA will accept both Provisional and Substantive Maintenance Orders of all descriptions, which of course, includes Affiliation Orders.

NEW BRUNSWICK will not accept Affiliation Orders, whether Provisional or Substantive.

ALBERTA will not accept Provisional Affiliation Orders with a view to holding confirmation proceedings in that Province, but will, nevertheless, accept for registration and enforcement a Substantive Affiliation Order which has already been made by due process of law in a United Kingdom Court where both parties have had the opportunity of being heard in the proceedings in the United Kingdom.

APPENDIX "C"

Countries to which Part II of the Maintenance Orders (Reciprocal Enforcement) Act 1972 applies.

CONVENTION COUNTRIES

Note (1) All documents to be transmitted via the Home Office,
(2) Sums collected by the Justices' Clerk to be sent to such person or authority as directed by the Secretary of State.

Name of Country	**Also, Reciprocating Country under:-**
ALGERIA	—
AUSTRIA	—
BARBADOS	Part I of 1972 Act. (Appendix "B")
BELGIUM	—
BRAZIL	—
CENTRAL AFRICAN REPUBLIC	—
CHILE	—
CZECHOSLOVAKIA	Hague Convention
DENMARK	—
ECUADOR	—
FINLAND	Hague Convention
FRANCE	Hague Convention, for France only.
(including Guadeloupe, Guiana, Martinique, Reunion, Camoro Archipelago, French Polynesia, Territory of the Afars and Isaacs, New Caledonia and Dependencies, St. Pierre and Miquelon)	—
GERMANY (Federal Republic of, and WEST BERLIN)	—
GREECE	—
GUATEMALA	—
HAITI	—
HOLY SEE	—
HUNGARY	—
ISRAEL	—
ITALY	Hague Convention
LUXEMBOURG	Hague Convention
MONACO	—
MOROCCO	—
NETHERLANDS (Kingdom in Europe and Netherlands Antilles)	Hague Convention
NIGER	—
NORWAY	Hague Convention
PAKISTAN	—
PHILLIPINES	—
POLAND	—
PORTUGAL	Hague Convention
SPAIN	—

SRI LANKA	Appendix "A" (1920 Act)
SURINAME	—
SWEDEN	Hague Convention
SWITZERLAND	Hague Convention
TUNISIA	—
TURKEY	Hague Convention
UPPER VOLTA	—
YUGOSLAVIA	—
UNITED STATES OF AMERICA (see list of Convention States in Appendix "D" and notes on special procedure to be adopted. Paragraph 90 ante)	—

Additions

APPENDIX "D"

List of States in the United States of America to which Part II of the Maintenance Orders (Reciprocal Enforcement) Act 1972 applies, subject to modification in so far as it affects cases prepared in the United Kingdom for transmission to those States.

ARIZONA
ARKANSAS
CALIFORNIA
COLORADO
CONNECTICUT
DELAWARE
FLORIDA
IDAHO
ILLINOIS
INDIANA
KANSAS
KENTUCKY
LOUISIANA
MAINE
MARYLAND
MASSACHUSETTS
MICHIGAN
MINNESOTA
MISSOURI
MONTANA
NEBRASKA
NEVADA
NEW HAMPSHIRE
NEW MEXICO
NEW YORK
NORTH CAROLINA
NORTH DAKOTA
OHIO
OKLAHOMA
OREGON
PENNSYLVANIA

RHODE ISLAND
SOUTH DAKOTA
TENNESSEE
TEXAS
UTAH
VERMONT
VIRGINIA
WASHINGTON
WISCONSIN
WYOMING

Additions

FORM 1

Summons to Respondent to show cause why Provisional Order should not be confirmed.

COUNTY OF

MAGISTRATES' COURT

To
of

WHEREAS application has been made to the   Court held at
in the Province/State/Republic of
under the provisions of the   Act, (being
an Act of the said Province/State/Republic)
by
of
(hereinafter called the Applicant) who states that she, the Applicant, is entitled to claim financial relief from you on the ground(s) that

AND WHEREAS on the   day of   19
UPON HEARING the evidence adduced in support of the said Application, the said Court, being satisfied that the applicant is entitled to the benefit of the above cited Act,
ORDERED AS FOLLOWS:
1. That you shall pay (here recite the terms of the Provisional Order)
2. That the said Order is PROVISIONAL ONLY and of no force or effect until confirmed by a competent Court in the Reciprocal State in which you reside. AND the said Provisional Order having been transmitted to this Court in accordance with (s.4 of the Maintenance Orders (Facilities for Enforcement) Act 1920) or (s.7 of the Maintenance Orders (Reciprocal Enforcement) Act 1972) (as the case may be)
A statement of the grounds on which the making of the Order might have been opposed under the law of the originating Reciprocal State is annexed hereto.

YOU ARE THEREFORE HEREBY SUMMONED to appear before the Magistrates' Court sitting at
on   day, the   day of   19   , at   a.m./p.m
TO SHOW CAUSE why the said Provisional Order should not be confirmed, without alteration, or with such alteration as the Court considers reasonable in the circumstances.

Dated this   day of   19

JUSTICES' CLERK

Note: A copy of the evidence adduced overseas in support of the Provisional Order will be supplied to you or your Solicitor on request. You should apply immediately to the Clerk to the Justices at

FORM 2

Confirmation of Provisional Order made in Reciprocating Country.

COUNTY OF

MAGISTRATES' COURT

WHEREAS application was made to the   Court
held at
in the Province/State/Republic of
under the provisions of the   Act,
(being an Act of the said Province/State/Republic)
by
of
(hereinafter called the applicant) that she, the applicant, is entitled to claim
financial relief from
of
(hereinafter called the defendant) on the ground(s) that

AND WHEREAS on the   day of   19   UPON HEARING
the evidence adduced in support of the said application, the said Court, being
satisfied that the applicant is entitled to the benefit of the above cited Act,
ORDERED AS FOLLOWS:
1. (here recite the financial provisions as set out in the Provisional Order)
2. That the said Order is PROVISIONAL ONLY and of no force or effect until
    confirmed by a competent court in the Reciprocal State in which the
    defendant resides.
    AND the said Provisional Order having been transmitted to this Court in
    accordance with (Section 4 of the Maintenance Orders (Facilities for
    Enforcement) Act 1920) or (Section 7 of the Maintenance Orders
    (Reciprocal Enforcement) Act 1972) (as the case may be)
UPON HEARING THE DEFENDANT/UPON PROOF THAT THE
DEFENDANT HAD BEEN DULY SERVED WITH A SUMMONS AND
THE DEFENDANT NOT HAVING APPEARED IN ANSWER THERETO/
    IT IS HEREBY ORDERED that the said PROVISIONAL ORDER be
confirmed as follows:-

    (here recite the financial provisions as set out in the Provisional Order,
    taking into account any alteration thereto as determined by the Justices,
    and expressing the amount payable in Sterling) (The order must contain a
    direction that payments be made through the Clerk to the Justices)
             Dated this   day of   19
             By Order of the Court,

             Justices' Clerk

Provisional Order made by a Magistrates' Court in England or Wales against a Respondent residing in a Reciprocating Country.

COUNTY OF

MAGISTRATES' COURT

BEFORE THE MAGISTRATES' COURT SITTING AT
on the   day of   19
APPLICATION having been made by
of
(hereinafter called the Applicant) under the provisions of the Domestic Proceedings and Magistrates' Courts Act 1978 and (Section 3 of the Maintenance Orders (Facilities for Enforcement) Act 1920) or (Part 1 of the Maintenance Orders (Reciprocal Enforcement) Act 1972) (as the case may be) for a MAINTENANCE ORDER against her husband, namely,

of
(hereinafter called the defendant) on the grounds that

being grounds upon which a Magistrates' Court in England and Wales is empowered to make a Maintenance Order within the meaning of the above cited Acts.
AND IT HAS BEEN PROVED that the defendant is now resident at the address set out above, being in a Country to which the last-mentioned Act extends, namely, the Province/State/Republic of
IT IS ADJUDGED that the Complaint is true, and pursuant to s.2 of the Domestic Proceedings and Magistrates' Courts Act 1978, IT IS ORDERED that the said
being the defendant, shall:
1.   Pay to the Applicant the monthly/weekly sum of
Sterling, for her benefit, during their joint lives, or until the Applicant shall re-marry;
2.   Pay to the child of the family named
who was born on the   day of   19   the weekly/monthly sum of   Sterling for the benefit of that child until that child attains the age of seventeen years;
3.   Pay to the child of the family named
who was born on the   day of   19   the weekly/monthly sum of   Sterling for the benefit of that child until that child attains the age of seventeen years;

IT IS FURTHER ORDERED that the said payments shall be made by the defendant to the Clerk to the Justices at
and the said Clerk to the Justices shall, upon receipt of the same,
1.   Pay the sums so received for the Applicant's benefit to the Applicant;
2.   Pay the sums so received for the benefit of each child to the Applicant for so long as each child shall respectively have his or her home with the applicant; and thereafter to such person with whom each child respectively has his or her home.

AND IT IS FURTHER ORDERED that the sums be payable by the defendant to the said Clerk to the Justices on the   day of each month/or/weekly on each Monday.

(THIS ORDER IS MADE PROVISIONALLY pursuant to/Section 3 of the Maintenance Orders (Facilities for Enforcement) Act 1920/Section 3 of the Maintenance Orders (Reciprocal Enforcement) Act 1972/and shall have no effect unless and until confirmed by a competent Court in (the Republic of South Africa) (the Province of British Columbia) (or as the case may be)

or

(THIS ORDER IS MADE PROVISIONALLY pursuant to Section 3 of the Maintenance Orders (Reciprocal Enforcement) Act 1972 (as modified by the Reciprocal Enforcement of Maintenance Orders (Republic of Ireland) Order 1974 and shall have no effect unless and until confirmed by this Court).

Dated this   day of   19

By Order of the Court,

JUSTICES' CLERK

I HEREBY CERTIFY that this is a true copy of the Order made in this matter now lawfully in my possession.

Dated this   day of   19

JUSTICES' CLERK

The above Order should be adapted where the Application is under the Guardianship of Minors Acts, the Affiliation Proceedings Act, or as the circumstances require.

FORM 4

DOMESTIC PROCEEDINGS AND MAGISTRATES' COURTS ACT 1978. (MAINTENANCE ORDERS (FACILITIES FOR ENFORCEMENT) ACT 1920) (MAINTENANCE ORDERS (RECIPROCAL ENFORCEMENT) ACT 1972. PART 1.)

....
(Applicant)

—v—

....
(Defendant)

The grounds upon which the making of the order in this matter might have been opposed if the defendant had been duly served with a summons, and had appeared at the hearing, are:

1. The Court has no jurisdiction to make the order.
2. The matter of the complaint is not true.
3. There is no valid marriage subsisting between the applicant and the defendant.
4. (a) A decree of judicial separation, or an order having the like effect, is in force.

    (b) Under a decree or order of a competent court legally enforceable in the United Kingdom, the applicant is already entitled to alimony and that such an order is being complied with.
5. In determining the amount of financial provision, if any, to be made by the defendant for the benefit of the applicant, the court is required to have regard to the following matters:-

    (a) the income, earning capacity, property and other financial resources which each of the parties to the marriage has or is likely to have in the foreseeable future;

    (b) the financial needs, obligations and responsibilities which each of the parties to the marriage has, or is likely to have, in the foreseeable future;

    (c) the standard of living enjoyed by the parties to the marriage before the occurrence of the conduct which is alleged as the ground of the application;

    (d) the age of each party to the marriage and the duration of the marriage;

    (e) any physical or mental disability of either of the parties to the marriage;

    (f) the contributions made by each of the parties to the welfare of the family, including any contribution made by looking after the home or caring for the family;

    (g) any other matter which in the circumstances of the case the court may consider relevant, including, so far as it is just to take it into account, the conduct of each of the parties in relation to the marriage;

and the defendant is entitled to rely on all or any of these matters to contend that the court should award a lesser amount of maintenance for the benefit of the complainant than it would otherwise have ordered, or no maintenance at all.

6. In determining the amount of financial provision, if any, to be made by the defendant for the benefit of any child of the family, the court is required to have regard to the following matters:-

    (a) the financial needs of the child;

    (b) the income, earning capacity (if any), property and other financial resources of the child;

(c) any physical or mental disability of the child

(d) the standard of living enjoyed by the family before the occurrence of the conduct which is alleged as the ground of the application;

(e) the manner in which the child was being and in which the parties to the marriage expected him to be educated or trained;

(f) the matters mentioned in relation to the parties in paras. (a) and (b) of Paragraph 5 above;

and the defendant is entitled to rely upon these criteria to contend that the court should award a smaller contribution towards the maintenance of the child than it would otherwise have ordered, or none at all.

7.   Where the child of the family is not a child of the applicant and the defendant, the defendant is entitled to contend that he has not treated the child as a child of the family, and that therefore no provision can be included in the order for the payment by him of maintenance for that child. "Child of the family" in relation to the parties to a marriage means:

(a) a child of both those parties, and

(b) any other child, not being a child who is boarded out with those parties by a local authority or voluntary organisation, who has been treated by both of those parties as a child of their family.

8.   Where the child of the family is not a child of the applicant and the defendant, the court, in determining the amount of financial provision, if any, to be made by the defendant for the benefit of that child, shall, in addition to the matters contained in para. 6 hereof, have regard to the following matters:

(a) to whether the defendant had assumed any responsibility for the child's maintenance and, if he did, to the extent to which, and the basis on which he assumed that responsibility, and to the length of time during which he discharged that responsibility;

(b) to whether in assuming and discharging that responsibility, the defendant did so knowing that the child was not his own child;

(c) to the liability of any other person to maintain the child;

and the defendant is entitled to rely upon these criteria in contending that the court should award a lesser contribution towards the maintenance of that child than it would otherwise have ordered, or none at all.

9.   (a) The child being over the age of 18 years, no financial provision can be included in the order for its maintenance except when the child will continue to be educated or trained, or any other special circumstances exist.

(b) The Court should not exercise its discretion to include, in the first instance, provision in the order for the maintenance of any child beyond its seventeenth birthday, because no sufficient circumstances exist which would justify the court including financial provision in the order for the child's benefit beyond its seventeenth birthday and ending on a date not beyond its eighteenth birthday.

10.   That the court should exercise its discretion by including in the order a date when the provision therein for the maintenance of the applicant shall cease.

11.   That the ground of the complaint has not been proved to the satisfaction of the court; therefore, provision should only be made in the order for the maintenance of any child of the family who is under the age of 18 years, bearing in mind the criteria set out in paras. 6, 8 and 9 hereof.

12.   Where the matter of complaint is alleged to be desertion;

(1) that the parting was by mutual consent;

(2) that the applicant's conduct gave the defendant just and reasonable cause for leaving;

(3) that the defendant has made a genuine offer to return to the applicant, and that such offer to return has been refused by the applicant without good cause.

DATED this   day of   19

Clerk to the Justices

Note: This form has been designed for use where proceedings are brought under the Domestic Proceedings and Magistrates' Courts Act 1978. It may be suitably adapted where proceedings are brought under the Guardianship of Minors Acts, the Affiliation Proceedings Act or any other enactment.

FORM 5

HOME OFFICE RECOMMENDED FORM

(For use in proceedings in all countries set out in Appendix "C", except U.S.A. or when proceedings are instituted under the Hague Convention arrangements)

WIFE MAINTENANCE.
CHILD MAINTENANCE.

APPLICATION FOR THE RECOVERY OF MAINTENANCE FROM A PERSON SUBJECT TO THE JURISDICTION OF A STATE WHICH IS A CONTRACTING PARTY TO THE UNITED NATIONS CONVENTION ON THE RECOVERY ABROAD OF MAINTENANCE.

......................................Court
....
....

England and Wales/Scotland/Northern Ireland.

In the matter of
......................................Claimant
against
......................................Respondent

1.   The claim of ....
                             (state name of claimant)
who states that she is married to the said respondent and that she resides at ....
....
in the County of ....

2.   That the claimant is the mother and the said respondent is the father of the following dependant child(ren):

1.................................born......................
2.................................born......................
3.................................born......................
4.................................born......................

3.   That the claimant is entitled to and seeks the recovery of maintenance from the said respondent for ....
....
....
(state whether maintenance sought for self, for child(ren) or for both)
in the weekly amount of £..
....
....
(state separate amounts for self and for individual child(ren), if maintenance sought for both)
4.   That upon information and belief the respondent is now residing at ....
....
in the State of ....
and is subject to the jurisdiction of that State, which is a Contracting Party to the United Nations Convention on the Recovery Abroad of Maintenance done at New York on 20 June 1956.
WHEREFORE, the claimant applies for such an order of maintenance directed to the said respondent as shall be deemed fair and reasonable.
5.   Evidence in support of this application is attached.
6.   The following documents are also attached:
        (1) an authority for the Receiving Agency in the said State to take on the claimant's behalf all appropriate steps for the recovery of maintenance:
        (2) documents establishing the family relationship of the claimant and respondent and their relationship to any dependant child(ren): namely: (list documents exhibited) ·
        ....
        ....
        ....
        ....
        (3) a photograph of the claimant/and a photograph of the respondent/ (delete if none available)
        (4) other documents as follows ....
        ....
        ....
        ....

(signed)...
(Claimant)
Taken before me this .... day of 19

Justice of the Peace/Justices' Clerk.

FORM 6

HOME OFFICE RECOMMENDED FORM
(for use in proceedings in all countries set out in Appendix "C" except U.S.A. or when proceedings are instituted under the Hague Convention arrangements)

AFFILIATION

APPLICATION FOR THE RECOVERY OF MAINTENANCE FROM A PERSON SUBJECT TO THE JURISDICTION OF A STATE WHICH IS A CONTRACTING PARTY TO THE UNITED NATIONS CONVENTION ON THE RECOVERY OF MAINTENANCE ABROAD.

....Court
....

England and Wales/Scotland/Northern Ireland

In the matter of
....Claimant
against
....Respondent

1.   The claim of ....
(state name of claimant)
who states that she is a single woman and that she resides at ....
....
in the County of ....
2.   That the claimant is the mother and the said respondent is the putative father of the following dependent child(ren):

1..born on................................
2..born on................................
3..born on................................

3.   That the claimant is entitled to and seeks the recovery of maintenance from the said respondent for the said child(ren) in the weekly amount of £.................
4.   That upon information and belief the respondent is now residing at.............
....
in the State of .... and is subject to the jurisdiction of that State, which is a Contracting Party to the United Nations Convention on the Recovery Abroad of Maintenance done at New York on 20 June 1956.
WHEREFORE, the claimant applies for such an order of maintenance directed to the said respondent as shall be deemed fair and reasonable.
5.   Evidence in support of this application is attached.
6.   The following documents are also attached:
(1) an authority for the Receiving Agency in the said State to take on the claimant's behalf all appropriate steps for the recovery of maintenance.
(2) a photograph of the claimant/and a photograph of the respondent (delete if none available)
(3) other documents as follows ....

....
....
....

(signed) ....
(Claimant)

Taken before me this .... day of 19

Justice of the Peace / Justices' Clerk.

FORM 7

HOME OFFICE RECOMMENDED FORM
(for use in conjunction with Form 5 and Form 6)

EVIDENCE IN SUPPORT OF APPLICATION FOR RECOVERY OF
MAINTENANCE UNDER UNITED NATIONS CONVENTION.

....Court
....
....

In the matter of

....Claimant
against
....Respondent

.... the claimant,
being duly sworn, gives evidence as follows:
1.   What is your full name, date of birth and nationality?

2.   Where do you reside?

3.   What is the full name and address of your legal representative in the United
Kingdom, if you have one?

4.   ANSWER ONLY IF YOU HAVE AT ANY TIME BEEN MARRIED TO
THE RESPONDENT
When and where were you married to the respondent?

Are you still the wife of the respondent?
When did the respondent last live with you?

Were any children born of this marriage; adopted during the marriage; or accepted as members of the family during the marriage? If so, state the names, ages and dates of birth of the children and whether they were born of the marriage, adopted during the marriage or accepted as members of the family during the marriage?
1.
2.
3.
4.
Which of these child(ren) are financially dependent on you?

Are you claiming maintenance from the respondent for yourself, for one or more children or for yourself and child(ren)? List the persons for whom maintenance is claimed.
1.
2.
3.
4.
What, briefly, are the grounds for your claim?

When did the respondent last make a contribution towards the maintenance of the persons for whom maintenance is claimed?

Have you applied to any other court for a maintenance order for yourself and/or for any of the said children? If so, has any maintenance order been made? (Attach copy of any order together with any certificate or arrears if order was made by a court in the United Kingdom).

What is the amount of maintenance you are claiming from the respondent for yourself and/or any of the said children?

5. ANSWER ONLY IF YOU ARE SEEKING MAINTENANCE FOR CHILDREN BORN OUT OF WEDLOCK.
Is the respondent the putative father of any of your children born out of wedlock?

If so, what are their names, ages and dates of birth?
1.
2.
3.
4.
Has the paternity of these children been determined by any Court? If so, when and by which Court? (Attach copy of any Order)

If paternity has not been determined by a Court, have you evidence to support your allegation that the respondent is the putative father of these children? (Attach any such evidence)

Has the respondent made any contribution to you for the maintenance of these children? If so, when was the last time?

Have you applied to any other Court for an order for maintenance of any of these children? If so, has any order been made? (Attach copy of order, together with any certificate of arrears if order was made by a Court in the United Kingdom).

What is the amount of maintenance you are claiming from the respondent for these children?

6.   Are you receiving assistance from the Supplementary Benefits Commission? If so, in what amount?

7.   Are you employed and, if so, where? What is your occupation if you are not employed?

8.   What is your present weekly "take home" pay (including overtime)?

9.   Are you in business on your own account? If so, state the nature of business and the last year's net profit.

10.   Do you receive a weekly income from any of the following sources? If so, state the amount received.
     Family allowance
     National Insurance Benefit
     Disability pension
     Service pension
     Superannuation
     Old age pension

11.   Do you have any other source of income? If so, what and in what amount?

12.   What do you spend each week to support yourself and your children?
     Rent (including rates if payable by you)
     Mortgage repayments (including rates)
     Household expenses (i.e. gas, electricity etc.)
     Food
     Household supplies
     Clothes
     Hire purchase payments
     School fees
     School meals
     Travelling expenses
     Insurance premiums

Incidental expenses
Other

TOTAL

13.   So far as you know, what is the respondent's full name, date of birth and nationality?

14.   Can you describe the respondent? (You should attach a photograph of him if you have one)
Height
Hair
Eyes
Other distinguishing marks (e.g. moustache, scars, etc)

15.   ANSWER TO THE BEST OF YOUR KNOWLEDGE AND BELIEF
What is the respondent's present address?

At which other addresses, if any, has the respondent lived during the past five years?
1.
2.
3.
What is the respondent's usual occupation?

Is the respondent employed and, if so, where? What is his salary?

Does the respondent have any additional income?

Does the respondent own property in any country?

Does the respondent maintain any other dependants?

(signed)..
Claimant.

Sworn before me this   day of   19

Justice of the Peace / Justices' Clerk.

93

FORM OF AUTHORITY

I, the undersigned ....
(state full name)

of...
(state full address)

HEREBY EMPOWER ....

....
(to be completed by the Home Office)

to take, on my behalf, all appropriate steps for the recovery of maintenance from

....
(state name of respondent)

including the settlement of the claim and, where necessary, the institution and prosecution of an action for maintenance and the execution of any order or other judicial act for the payment of maintenance.

Drawn up at ....

on ....

....
(signature)

As witnessed by ....

FORM 8

HOME OFFICE RECOMMENDED FORM

(For use in proceedings where the respondent is residing in the United States of America)

PETITION FOR SUPPORT

.... (Magistrates' Court (Code   )

In the matter of

....Petitioner

against

....Respondent

1.   The petition of ....
respectfully shows that she is the
      (a) wife of the above named respondent, or
      (b) former wife of the above named respondent, or
      (c) mother of a child/children of which the above named respondent is the putative father
               (delete (a) (b) or (c) above as appropriate)

2. That your petitioner is the mother and the said respondent is the father of the following named dependants:

1... born on ....
2... born on ....
3... born on ....
4... born on ....
5... born on ....
6... born on ....

3. That the petitioner and the said children are in need of and entitled to support from the respondent under the provisions of Part II of the Maintenance Orders (Reciprocal Enforcement) Act 1972, a copy of which is attached hereto and made a part hereof.

4. That the respondent on or about .... and subsequent thereto refused fully and neglected to provide fair and reasonable support for the petitioner and his dependants according to his means and earning capacity.

5. That upon information and belief the respondent is now residing at or is domiciled at ....
....

WHEREFORE, the petitioner prays for an order for support directed to the said respondent as shall be deemed fair and reasonable, and for such other and further relief as the law provides.

6. Testimony in support of this petition is attached hereto and made a part hereof.

....
(Petitioner)

Address ....
....
....

....being duly sworn, deposes and says: That she is the petitioner herein and that she has read the foregoing petition and knows the contents thereof and that the same is true of her own knowledge except as to the matters therein stated to be alleged on information and belief, and as to those matters she believes it to be true.

....
(Petitioner)

TAKEN ON OATH before me on the   day of   19

(Court
Stamp)   Justice of the Peace

I ....clerk of the said Court, hereby certify that .... whose genuine signature is subscribed to the foregoing, was at the time of signing a justice of the peace for the county of.................................. in which county sits the aforesaid court.

Dated the   day of   19

Justices' Clerk.

(Court Stamp)

FORM 9

HOME OFFICE RECOMMENDED FORM
(for use in conjunction with Form 8)

TESTIMONY

.... Magistrates' Court (Code   )

.... Petitioner

against

.... Respondent

.... the petitioner herein,
being duly sworn, testifies as follows:-

1.   Q. What is your full name, date of birth and nationality?
       A.

2.   Q. Where do you reside?
       A.

3.   Q. What is the full name and address of your legal representative in the United Kingdom, if you have one?
       A.

4. ANSWER ONLY IF YOU HAVE AT ANY TIME BEEN MARRIED
TO THE RESPONDENT
Q. When and where were you married to the respondent?
A.

Q. Are you still the wife of the respondent?
A.
Q. When did the respondent last live with you?
A.
Q. Were any children born of this marriage; adopted during the marriage;
or accepted as members of the family during the marriage? If so, state the
names, ages and dates of birth of the children and whether they were born
of the marriage, adopted during the marriage or accepted as members of
the family during the marriage?

A. 1...
   2...
   3...
   4...

Q. Which of these child(ren) are financially dependent on you?
A.

Q. Are you claiming maintenance from the respondent for yourself, for
one or more children or for yourself and child(ren)? List the persons for
whom maintenance is claimed.
A. 1...
   2...
   3...
   4...

Q. What, briefly, are the grounds for your claim?
A.

Q. When did the respondent last make a contribution towards the
maintenance of the persons for whom maintenance is claimed, and what
was the amount of the contribution?
A.

Q. Have you applied to any other court for a maintenance order for
yourself and/or for any of the said children? If so, has any maintenance
order been made? (Attach copy of any order together with particulars of
any arrears)
A.

Q. What is the amount of maintenance you are claiming from the respondent for yourself and/or each of the said children? If children are of working age explain why they are not working. If the amount requested is at variance with the amount awarded under an existing order, explain why.
A. Self..

Children 1..
         2..
         3..
         4..

5. ANSWER ONLY IF YOU ARE SEEKING MAINTENANCE FOR CHILDREN BORN OUT OF WEDLOCK.
Q. Is the respondent the putative father of any of your children born out of wedlock?
A.

Q. If so, what are their names, ages and dates of birth?
A. 1..
   2..
   3..
   4..

Q. Has the paternity of these children been determined by any Court? If so, when and by which Court? (Attach copy of any Order)
A.

Q. If paternity has not been determined by a Court, have you evidence to support your allegation that the respondent is the putative father of these children? (Attach any such evidence)
A.

Q. Has the respondent made any contribution to you for the maintenance of these children? If so, when was the last time and what was the amount?
A.

Q. Have you applied to any other Court for an Order for maintenance of any of these children? If so, has any order been made? (Attach copy of order, together with particulars of any arrears)
A.

Q. What is the amount of maintenance you are claiming from the respondent for each of these children? If children are of working age explain why they are not working. If the amount requested is at variance with the amount awarded under an existing order explain why.
A. 1..
   2..

3...
4...

6. Q. Are you receiving assistance from the Supplementary Benefits Commision? If so, in what amount?
    A.

7. Q. Are you employed and, if so, where? What is your occupation if you are not employed?
    A.

8. Q. What is your present weekly "take home" pay (including overtime?)
    A.

9. Q. Are you in business on your own account? If so, state nature of business and the last year's net profit.
    A.

10. Q. Do you receive a weekly income from any of the following sources? If so, state the amount received.

    Child benefit...
    National Insurance benefit...
    Disability pension..
    Service pension...
    Superannuation ....
    Old age pension..

11. Q. Do you have any other sources of income? If so, what and in what amount?
    A.

12. Q. What do you spend each week to support yourself and your children?
    Rent (including rates if payable by you)..........................
    Mortgage repayments (including rates)...........................
    Household expenses (i.e. gas, electricity etc.)...................
    Food ....
    Household supplies...
    Clothes ....
    Hire purchase payments...
    School fees...
    School meals...
    Travelling expenses..

Insurance premiums...

Incidental expenses...

Other ....

....

TOTAL   ....

13.   Q. So far as you know, what is the resondent's:-
       A. Full name...
          Date of Birth..
          Nationality ....
          U.S. Social Security number (if known)................................

14.   Q. Can you describe the respondent? (You should attach a photograph of
       him if you have one)
       A. Height ....
          Hair ....
          Eyes ....
          Other distinguishing marks (e.g. moustache, scars, etc.)................
          ....
          ....

15.   ANSWER TO THE BEST OF YOUR KNOWLEDGE AND BELIEF
       Q. What is the respondent's present address?
       A.

       Q. At which other addresses, if any, has the respondent lived during the
       past 5 years?
       A. 1...
          2...
          3...

       Q. What is the respondent's usual occupation?
       A.

       Q. Is the respondent employed and if so, where? What is his salary?
       A.

       Q. Does the respondent have any additional income?
       A.

       Q. Does the respondent own property in any country?
       A.

       Q. Does the respondent maintain any other dependants?
       A.

16.   Q. Did you ever reside in the United Kingdom with the respondent?
       A.

....
Petitioner.

TAKEN ON OATH before me on ....

Justice of the Peace.

PAUPER'S AFFIDAVIT

.... Magistrates' Court (Code   )
In the matter of a proceeding under the Maintenance Orders (Reciprocal
Enforcement) Act 1972.

....Petitioner

against

....Respondent

I... hereby state that I am the
petitioner in the above entitled proceedings and pray that proceedings be
instituted in the .... Court of the State
of..................................... in and for the County of ....
for an Order of Support and/or Reimbursement of support against ....
.... and that I am financially unable to pay any costs or fees which are
incurred in the said proceedings

....
Petitioner

TAKEN ON OATH before me on..

Justice of the Peace.

FORM 10

HOME OFFICE RECOMMENDED FORM
(This form must accompany forms 8 and 9)

CERTIFICATE

....Magistrates' Court (Code   )

....Petitioner

against

....Respondent

I HEREBY CERTIFY:-

1. That on .... 19......... an application was made to this Court in the form entitled Petition for Support by the Petitioner under the provisions of the Maintenance Orders (Reciprocal Enforcement) Act 1972 for the purpose of recovering maintenance from the respondent for the petitioner and any other person named in the petition.

2. That it appears to the Court that the respondent is residing at ...., City of .... State of..

3. That according to the statement of the petitioner the needs of the dependent(s) named in the said petition for support from the respondent are the sum of .... per ....

4. That the petition sets forth facts from which it may be determined that the respondent owes a duty to maintain the petitioner and any other person named in the petition and that a Court in the State of .... may obtain jurisdiction of the respondent or his property.

5. That in the opinion of the undersigned, the respondent should be compelled to answer such petition and be dealt with according to Law.

Dated the....................day of.............................19..........

Justice of the Peace.

FORM 10A

PRESCRIBED FORM
FORM OF NOTICE UNDER S.35(4) OF THE MAINTENANCE ORDERS (RECIPROCAL ENFORCEMENT) ACT 1972.

....Magistrates' Court (Code   )

Date   :
To the Defendant :
of   :
                           Complaint has been made by
The Complainant :

102

of   :

who states that by an order made on.......................................
under the ....Act
     by the ....Magistrates' Court,
YOU WERE ORDERED AS FOLLOWS:-

and applies for that order to be/revoked/varied by an order requiring

on the ground that

Date of hearing : The hearing of the Complaint will be on ....
.... at   m. at ....
....................................Magistrates' Court

Justices' Clerk.

Note: If you do not appear at the time and place specified above the Court may proceed in your absence. If you wish to make written representations to the Court you may do so on the enclosed form.

Important: The date fixed for the hearing must not be earlier than SIX WEEKS after this notice is sent to the Home Office with a view to service thereof. (See paragraph 87 of the Guide)

FORM 11

HOME OFFICE RECOMMENDED FORM

NOTICE TO PAYER THAT PROVISIONAL MAINTENANCE ORDER
HAS BEEN MADE.

To
of
in the Republic of Ireland.

....Magistrates' Court.

ON THE COMPLAINT OF

of

that (here set out grounds of complaint)

the court on the .... day of 19
made a provisional order ordering you, the above named defendant, to pay the
following sums weekly/monthly; namely the sum of £   for the benefit
of ....
....

       I hereby give you notice that:-
       (1)   the provisional order has no effect unless and until it has been
       confirmed by the court;
       (2)   the order may be confirmed with or without alteration;
       (3)   in considering whether or not to confirm the order the court will
       take into account any representations made by you or any evidence
       adduced by you which reach the court within three weeks from the
       date on which this notice is served on you.
If you intend to defend or be represented at the hearing to consider whether or not
to confirm the order, you should fill in and sign the attached form of defence and
send it by prepaid registered post to me at ....
.... before the expiration of ten days from the date
of service of this notice upon you.
You may defend the proceedings in person or be legally represented at the
hearing. Legal aid is available if you wish to be represented and if you are
financially eligible. I will arrange for a form of application for legal aid to be sent
to you by the Law Society if you notify me of your wish.
If you wish to adduce evidence, but do not wish to attend the proceedings, the
evidence may be set out in an affidavit sworn before a solicitor in the Republic of
Ireland. If the affidavit is sent to me, I will produce it to the Court.
If you do not wish to defend the proceedings, but would like certain matters to be
brought to the attention of the court, which is considering whether or not to
confirm the provisional order, you may submit them to me and I will bring them to
the attention of the Court.
Whether or not you decide to defend or be represented in the proceedings, it will
be helpful to the court, in considering whether or not to confirm the order, to have
information about your income, resources and financial commitments. You
should therefore complete the attached "Statement of Means" and return it to
me.

      Dated ....

               ....

               Justices' Clerk.

FORM 12.

HOME OFFICE RECOMMENDED FORM
(To accompany Form 11)

FORM OF DEFENCE

This form should be completed and signed and returned to the Court by pre-paid registered post before the expiration of ten days from the date of service of the attached Notice.

I ....

of ....

intend to defend or be represented at the hearing to consider whether or not to confirm the provisional order made against me on the complaint of ....

....

..................................(insert name and address of complainant)

I wish/do not wish (delete as appropriate)

to apply for legal aid for the purpose of the proceedings. Further communications regarding these proceedings should be forwarded to me at............................

....

SIGNATURE ....

DATE ....

The Clerk to the Justices,
(address)

FORM 13.

HOME OFFICE RECOMMENDED FORM
(To accompany form 11)

STATMENT OF MEANS

This form should be completed and returned to the Court whether or not a form of defence is also completed and returned.

FULL NAME ....

INCOME

1. What is your weekly gross pay, including all overtime and bonuses? (Do not deduct income tax or any other deductions from your pay)   £

2. Do you receive any weekly income from the State (e.g. social security, pension)?   £

3. What is the weekly "take home" pay of all other persons living with you as part of your family?   £

4. If you have any other source(s) of income please give details £

EXPENDITURE

5. What deductions are made from your pay, e.g. in respect of income tax (Give details)   £

6. What do you and any other persons living with you as part of your family spend each week on the following items?

Rent (including rates if payable by you)	£
Mortgage repayments (including rates)	£
Household expenses (i.e. gas, electricity etc)	£
Food	£
Household supplies	£
Clothes	£
School fees	£
School meals	£
Court Orders (debts, maintenance etc)	£
Insurance premiums	£
Hire purchase payments	£
Travelling expenses	£
Other expenses (give details)	£
TOTAL	£

FORM 14

PRESCRIBED FORM.

NOTICE TO PAYER OF REGISTRATION OF MAINTENANCE ORDER
(Republic of Ireland)

To
of
(insert name and address of payer)

I HEREBY GIVE YOU NOTICE that on the   day of
19   I REGISTERED a Maintenance Order (copy attached) made by the
....Court in the Republic of Ireland ORDERING
YOU TO PAY .... (insert name and address
of payee) .... the sum of .... (insert amount and
period e.g. monthly) ....
       YOU ARE ENTITLED TO APPEAL to the ....
Magistrates' Court within one calendar month from the date of service of this
notice to set aside the registration of the order on one of the following grounds:-

(a)   that the registration is contrary to public policy;
(b)   if you did not appear in the proceedings in the Republic of Ireland, that you
were not served with the summons or other notice of the proceedings either in
sufficient time to enable you to arrange for your defence or in accordance with the
law of the place where you were residing;
(c)   that the order is irreconcilable with a judgement given in the United
Kingdom in proceedings between you and the above mentioned payee.

....
Justices' Clerk
(Address)

FORM 15

PRESCRIBED FORM

NOTICE TO PAYEE THAT MAINTENANCE ORDER HAS NOT BEEN REGISTERED (Republic of Ireland)

To:
of:
(insert name and address of payee)

       I HEREBY GIVE NOTICE that I have not registered a maintenance order
made by the ....
Court in the Republic of Ireland ordering...
.... (insert name and address of payer) ....
to pay you the sum of .... (insert amount and period e.g.
monthly) .... on the ground that ....(insert one of
the grounds specified in s.6(5) of the Maintenance Orders (Reciprocal
Enforcement) Act 1972) ....
       You are entitled to appeal against my decision to the ....
Magistrates' Court to have the Order registered.
       If you wish to appeal, you may do so by completing and returning to me the
notice of appeal set out below. Unless you are present in Court or legally

represented when the appeal is heard, the court may dismiss the case. If you wish to be legally represented, you may apply to ....
(insert the name and address of the Secretary of the appropriate legal aid commitee) .... for legal aid and advice.

Dated this   day of   19

Justices' Clerk
(address)

FORM 16

PRESCRIBED FORM (To accompany Form No.15)

MAINTENANCE ORDERS (RECIPROCAL ENFORCEMENT) ACT 1972.

APPEAL BY WAY OF COMPLAINT

....Magistrates' Court (Code   )

Date :
Defendant :
Address :

Matter of
Complaint :   The .... Court
at .... in the Republic
of Ireland having on ....
made a maintenance order requiring the defendant to pay to the
undersigned complainant the sum of £................... (weekly or
as the case may be) and the order having been sent to the Justices'
Clerk for the said Magistrates' Court for registration; the Justices'
Clerk has refused to register the order on the ground that...........
....
....
I HEREBY APPEAL to the said Magistrates' Court against the
refusal to register this order.

(Signed)...
(Complainant)

FORM 17

.... MAGISTRATES' COURT
COUNTY OF .... in ENGLAND/WALES.

DOMESTIC PROCEEDINGS AND MAGISTRATES' COURTS ACT 1978.
S.2. MAINTENANCE ORDERS (RECIPROCAL ENFORCEMENT) ACT
1972. Part 1.

NOTICE OF INSTITUTION OF PROCEEDINGS
(Hague Convention Countries)

To:
of:

YOU ARE HEREBY GIVEN NOTICE that proceedings have been instituted
against you in the above named Magistrates' Court by your wife, namely
....
of ....
(hereinafter called the Complainant), by way of complaint, WHEREBY the
Complainant seeks a MAINTENANCE ORDER against you requiring you to
pay such weekly sum for her benefit, together with such weekly sum for the
maintenance of each of the following children of the family, namely,
1... born on ....
2... born on ....
3... born on ....
4... born on ....
as the Court considers reasonable, on the following grounds:-
1 ....
....
2 ....
....
3 ....
....
Brief particulars of the evidence to be adduced by the Complainant at the hearing
of the proceedings are set out in the document annexed hereto.
If you wish to defend or be represented at the hearing of the proceedings you
should fill in and sign the attached "notice of defence/representations" and send it
by prepaid registered post to me at the Justices' Clerk's Office, ...
....
before the expiration of ten days from the date of the service of this notice upon
you.
You may appear at the proceedings in person or be legally represented at the
hearing, or you may do both, and also, if you wish, bring any witnesses whom you
may have with you to the Court. If you wish to be legally represented at the
proceedings and cannot afford to pay for your legal representation, legal aid may
be available to you, if you qualify financially. If you wish to apply for legal aid I
will arrange for a form of application for legal aid to be sent to you by the Law
Society if you notify me of your wish.
If you intend to deny the substance of the Complaint but cannot, or do not wish, to

attend at the Court, it is open to you to adduce evidence in your own Country in defence of the proceedings. Your evidence, and that of any witnesses whom you may have, may be set out in the form of an affidavit sworn before a Judge, Judicial Officer or Advocate of the Country where you reside. The affidavits should then be sent to me at the address given above. Any affidavits you send to me will be produced and read by me to the Court.

If you do not intend to defend the proceedings or to be legally represented at the hearing, it would be helpful to the Court if you would fill in and sign the attached statement of means so as to assist the Court in making a fair assessment of the amount you would be in a position to pay.

Also, if you would like certain matters to be brought to the attention of the Court (not being matters in defence of the proceedings) you may write them on the attached "Notice of Defence/Representations".

Even if you intend to defend the proceedings, it would be helpful to the Court to have information about your means.

Notice of the date fixed for the hearing of the proceedings will be sent to you in due course. The hearing will not take place earlier than six weeks from the date of service of this notice upon you.

Dated this .... day of ....19.........

Clerk to the Justices'
(Address —)
(Telephone No. —)

Note: This form may be adapted for use under ss. 6 & 7 of the Domestic Proceedings & Magistrates' Courts Act 1978, the Guardianship of Minors Acts, the Affiliation Proceedings Act 1957 and so on.

FORM 17 (Continued)

NOTICE OF DEFENCE/ REPRESENTATIONS

To: The Clerk to the Justices,
of:

I ....
of ....

(A) INTEND TO DEFEND or BE REPRESENTED at the hearing of the proceedings brought against me by ....
of ....

I attach hereto a statement of my means

or

(B) I DO NOT INTEND TO DEFEND THE PROCEEDINGS but would like the following matters to be brought to the attention of the Court:-

I attach a statement of my means.

Dated ....

Signed ....

Further communications should be sent to me at the following address ....

....

Note: Strike out "A" or "B" whichever does not apply.

An appropriate form of Statement of Means is given at Form 13.

FORM 18

.... MAGISTRATES' COURT

COUNTY OF .... in ENGLAND/WALES.

DOMESTIC PROCEEDINGS AND MAGISTRATES' COURTS ACT
1978. S.2. (or as the case may be)
MAINTENANCE ORDERS (RECIPROCAL ENFORCEMENT) ACT
1972. Part 1

NOTICE OF HEARING.
(Hague Convention Countries)

To:

of:

I HEREBY GIVE YOU NOTICE that the proceedings instituted against you by
your wife, namely ....

of ....

will be heard before the MAGISTRATES' COURT sitting at ....

....

on .... at   m. when you may either
attend in person, or be legally represented, or both, and also, if you wish, bring
any witnesses whom you may have.

IF YOU DO NOT WISH TO BE PRESENT, but intend to defend the
proceedings, you should let me have your sworn affidavits not later than
...., if you
have not already submitted them to me.

Dated ....

Clerk to the Justices.
(Address —   )
(Telephone —   )

FORM 19

PRESCRIBED FORM

To ....
.... (insert name and address of payer) ....
I hereby give notice that on .... day of .... 19..................
I registered a maintenance order (copy attached) made by the ....
.... Court in ....
.... (insert name of Hague Convention Country) ....
ordering you to pay .... (insert name of payee) ....
the sum of .... (insert amount in sterling and period e.g. monthly)
....

Your are entitled to appeal to the ....
Magistrates' Court within one calendar month from the date of the service of this
notice to set aside the registration of the order on one of the following grounds:-

    (a)   that the court making the order did not have jurisdiction to do so*

    (b)   that the registration is contrary to public policy;

    (c)   that the order was obtained by fraud in connection with a matter of procedure;

    (d)   that proceedings between you and the payee and having the same purpose are pending before a Court in the United Kingdom and those proceedings were instituted before these proceedings

    (e)   that the order is incompatible with a judgment given in proceedings between you and the payee and having the same purpose, either in the United Kingdom or in a Hague Convention Country.

    (f)   If you did not appear in the proceedings in the Hague Convention Country, that you were not given notice of the institution of the proceedings, including notice of the substance of the claim, in accordance with the law of that Country, and in sufficient time to enable you to defend the proceedings.

Dated...

Clerk of the Court.

* Note to Form 19.
Jurisdiction may be based —

    (a)   on the habitual residence of the payer or payee in that State.

    (b)   on the payer and the payee being nationals of that State,

    (c)   on your submission to the jurisdiction of the Court; or

    (d)   in the case of an order made on divorce etc., on any ground which is recognised by United Kingdom law.

FORM 20

PRESCRIBED FORM

Notice to payee that maintenance order has not been registered.

To ....
.........................(insert name and address of payee) ....

I hereby give notice that I have not registered a maintenance order made by
the ....Court in ....
...................(insert name of Hague Convention Country) ....
ordering ....(insert name and address of payer) ....
.... to pay you the sum of ....
..............(insert amount in sterling and period e.g. monthly) ....
on the ground that .... (insert one of the grounds specified in s.6(5),
(6) or (7) of the Maintenance Orders (Reciprocal Enforcement) Act 1972
(as extended by the Reciprocal Enforcement of Maintenance (Hague
Convention Countries) Order 1979).
You are entitled to appeal against my decision to the ....
Magistrates' Court within one calendar month from the date when this
notice was given to have the order registered.
If you wish to appeal, you may do so by completing and returning to me the
notice of appeal annexed hereto. Unless you are present in court or legally
represented when the appeal is heard the court may dismiss the case. If you
wish to be legally represented and need legal aid or advice you may apply to
the Area Secretary, the Law Society, 14 (London West) Legal Aid Area,
Area Headquarters, 29-37 Red Lion Street, London WC1R 4PP.

Dated.......................................

Clerk of the Court.

FORM 21

PRESCRIBED FORM
(This form to be annexed to Form 20)

MAINTENANCE ORDERS (RECIPROCAL ENFORCEMENT) ACT 1972.

Appeal by way of Complaint

.... Magistrates' Court (Code   )

Date:
Defendant:

Address:
Matter of
Complaint:

The ....Court

at ....

in ....

having on ....

made a maintenance order requiring the defendant to pay the undersigned complainant the sum of £.................... (weekly or as the case may be) and the order having been sent to the Justices' Clerk for the said Magistrates' Court for registration; the Justices' Clerk has refused to register the order on the ground that ....

....

....

I HEREBY APPEAL to the said Magistrates' Court against the refusal to register this Order.

(SIGNED) ....
(Complainant)

STATUTES REFERRED TO

INDEX

A Practical Guide to Magistrates' Courts'
Jurisdiction and Procedure in International
Domestic Proceedings.

USE OF INDEX

To determine the appropriate procedure, first trace the Country or Territory in the alphabetical lists in the Appendix "A", "B" or "C". If the name of the required Country or Territory is in

Appendix "A"   see under "Maintenance Orders (Facilities for Enforcement) Act 1920" in the index,

Appendix "B"   see under "Reciprocating Countries" in the index, unless referred to the separate section under the heading "Hague Convention Countries" by the appendix.

Appendix "C"   see under "Convention Countries". (Note the special modification for U.S.A. Individual States are noted in Appendix "D".)

For Scotland or Northern Ireland, see under "SCOTLAND AND NORTHERN IRELAND".

The Irish Republic is dealt with separately under the heading "IRELAND — REPUBLIC OF"

If the name of the overseas Country or Territory does not appear in any of the appendices, there were no reciprocal arrangements in existence at the date of publication of this Guide.

With the exception of the Forms, the numbers in the index refer to the appropriate paragraph in this Guide.

A

AFFILIATION ORDER

APPEAL

APPLICANT

ARREARS

B

BANK

BLOOD TEST

C

COMPLAINANT

CONVENTION COUNTRIES

E

EIRE

See under IRELAND — REPUBLIC OF

ENFORCEMENT

ENGLAND AND WALES

EVIDENCE

ADMISSIBILITY of, taken in

F

FORMS

H

HAGUE CONVENTION COUNTRIES

H

HIGH COURT

I

INTERIM ORDER

IRELAND — REPUBLIC OF

J

JUSTICES' CLERK

JUSTICES' REASONS

L

LEGAL AID

LUMP SUM ORDERS

M

MAINTENANCE ORDERS (FACILITIES FOR ENFORCEMENT) ACT 1920 (APPENDIX "A") COUNTRIES

MAINTENANCE ORDERS (GENERALLY)

MAINTENANCE ORDERS(RECIPROCAL ENFORCEMENT) ACT 1972

Part I — See under "Reciprocating Countries" and
Appendix "B"
Part I (Modified) — See under "Ireland — Republic of" or
"Hague Convention Countries" as case may be
Part II — See under "Convention Countries".
Part II (as modified for U.S.A.) — See under U.S.A.

N

NORTHERN IRELAND

See under "Scotland and Northern Ireland"

P

PAYEE

POWER OF ATTORNEY

PERIODICAL PAYMENTS

R

RECIPROCATING COUNTRIES
(under Part I of the Maintenance Orders (Reciprocal Enforcement) Act 1972)

REGISTRATION OF ORDERS

See under appropriate heading for Country or

Classification of Country required, e.g. Convention
Countries, Hague Convention Countries, Ireland —
Republic of, Reciprocating Countries, Scotland and
Northern Ireland

REVOCATION OF ORDERS

See under "Variation and Revocation of Orders" and also
under appropriate heading for Country or Classification of
Country required.

S

SCOTLAND AND NORTHERN IRELAND

132

W

WALES

Procedure as for England

WARRANT

of arrest — issue prohibited   6

WITNESS EXPENSES

Payment of   45,63,106,123

WITNESS SUMMONS

Power to issue   45,63